Essential Songwriter's
RHYMING
DICTIONARY

The most practical and easy-to-use reference now available

KEVIN M. MITCHELL

Alfred Music
Los Angeles

Library of Congress Cataloging-in-Publication Data

Mitchell, Kevin M., date.
Essential songwriter's rhyming dictionary: the most practical
and easy-to-use reference now available / Kevin M. Mitchell.
p. cm.
ISBN: 0-88284-729-5 (alk. paper)
1. English language—Rhyme—Dictionaries.
2. Popular music—Writing—and publishing. I. Title
PE1519.M5 1996
423'.1—dc20   96—32546
CIP

Cover photos: Corel Corp. (Railroad tracks: © PhotoDisc, Inc.)
Martin D-28 courtesy of the Martin Guitar Company
Fender Stratocaster courtesy of Fender Musical Instruments, Inc.

Piano photo: Jeff Oshiro

Table of Contents

Introduction

Words are the tools of the modern lyricist. This dictionary is your toolbox.

The *Essential Songwriter's Rhyming Dictionary* was developed with the contemporary songwriter in mind. Most words are cross-referenced in more than one place to make it quicker and easier to find the perfect word.

If you're trying to rhyme *antediluvian*, *odalisque* or *ubiquitous*, you won't find it in this book. Only the most often-used words of the modern song are listed here. Every editorial or formatting decision made was based on this image: it's late, you're sitting with pen in hand, and you've just written the perfect line—but you need something to rhyme with it, and you need it now. You grab this book, look up the word— and there are your rhymes. Inspired, you write the second perfect line, and on you go with your song.

This valuable toolbox of rhymes makes the development of your craft smooth and efficient. Use it to find the perfect word at just the right moment. Discover great words you've never thought of before.

I. How This Book Works

Traditional rhyming books take many pages to explain how to use their book—and even then, it's still hard to find your way around. Filled with references to "masculine" versus "feminine" rhymes, "penults" versus "antepenults," and "e" sounds versus "ee" sounds, they seem only usable by English professors. Others have headings like AK-*en*, IR-*up*, ÜR'*ning* (what's that mean?), etc. Before you can find your rhyme, you've lost your inspiration, if not your mind.

FORMAT

Formatting this dictionary was not without its challenges. Words are cross-referenced: if you want to rhyme *bad*, look up B*ad*, and you'll find *sad*. If you want to rhyme *sad*, look up S*ad*, and find *bad*, etc. However, there are over 400 words that rhyme with B*e*. To cross-reference them as previously described would create a volume roughly the size and weight of a cross-town bus.

In these instances, a "key word" was chosen (in this example, B*e*) and all the possible words rhyming with that were listed under the key word. So when you look up *Tea*, you find thisword. So when you look up *Tea*, you find this:

Tea (see **Be**).

That means that there are too many rhymes to list under all entries, and *Be* is the key word. Then, simply look up *Be*, and you'll find *Tea*, along with a few hundred common rhymes.

In the few instances where there are more than 100 rhymes for an entry, the words are grouped by syllable (one syllable, two syllable, etc.).

Remember the "key word" is often the most common, simplest word. So if you're trying to rhyme *oscillated*, and it's not listed, look up a simpler word which rhymes with it (like *hated*). Then look at that word—there you'll find all the words you need to rhyme with *oscillated*. This situation is rare indeed, but it's helpful to keep in mind if you're trying to rhyme a large word containing many syllables.

BROKEN RULES

Other rhyming dictionaries are too cumbersome for the contemporary songwriter. They have rigid rules of what rhymes, not taking into account different pronunciations or ways you can enunciate words to make them rhyme.

For example, under *Coffee* is only the word *toffee*. But in the world of pop music, *Be*, *Me*, etc., could work with *Coffee*. So when you see an entry that looks like this:

Coffee toffee (see *be*)

it means that toffee is all that rhymes with coffee, but if you look up *Be*, indicated in italic, you'll find other words that can work in a song. This "see" cross reference is also used when, depending on your dialect or accent, some other words are available that could possibly rhyme if pronounced in a certain way.

So when the word following "see" is in bold:

Among (see **Young**)

it means that the word is offered as a "strict" rhyme; when the referenced word is in italic, it is a suggestion of other possible rhymes.

Slang words and colloquialisms are included whenever possible and appropriate. Under the word *Anchor*, for example, you'll find *thank 'er*.

NAMES, PLACES, EXPRESSIONS, CLICHÉS

Names (*José*), famous people (*Sigmund Freud*) and places (*Trinidad*) are often included. These tend to be included when there were fewer rhymes in general, and was less likely to list them for words with many rhymes.

Common, everyday expressions and short clichés are also included wherever possible— and hopefully those listed will get you thinking of others that might be found in your corner of the world but aren't included here.

PREFIXES AND SUFFIXES

You can create more words by adding prefixes and suffixes. At the top of every dictionary page is a running header listing some of the most common prefixes and suffixes. When you're looking at a word, look up at the header, and mix and match what's there with the word you're looking at to create other words.

The more likely it is that a word could appear in a song, the more likely it's included in the initial list. (For example, under *View*, you'll find *review* and *preview*, etc.)

If you are trying to rhyme a word which has a prefix or suffix already built in and you don't find it, don't give up! You should find it in its original form. For example, if you're looking up *viewing*, and you don't find it, simply take off the suffix (in this case, *ing*), and look up *View*. There you'll find a list of words that only need the *"ing"* added to find the rhyme that's right for you.

WORDS LEFT OUT

In addition to words that would probably never be used in a song, a few common words were left out that had only one rhyme, if that rhyme was a word that would be extremely unusual in a pop song. For example, the only strict rhyme for *terminal* is *germinal*, which, according to *Merriam Webster's Collegiate Dictionary* means "relating to, or having the characteristic of a germ cell." This book assumes you're not, in fact, writing that great pop song about the heartache of being a germ.

Drug and sexual references are kept to a minimum. Obscene words and those words found offensive to particular ethnic groups or religions are also left out.

II. Glossary of Rhyme Schemes

Poetry is formed by a group of lines called a *stanza*, or scheme.

Many songwriters fall into a rut with regard to rhyme schemes—that is, using the same patterns over and over again. It's important to avoid this by learning and experimenting with as many rhyme schemes as possible to add variety and interest to your songs.

THE BASICS

Here are a few of the most common rhyme schemes found in poetry and songs all over the world. Letters (A, B, C, etc.) are used to notate the scheme (the recurrence of the rhyme).

A B C B

A

Roses are red

B

Violets are **blue**

C

Sugar is sweet

B

And so are **you**

Here are some variations on this format.

A B A B

      A
Roses are **red**
         B
Violets are **blue**
       A
I'm quite well-**fed**
       B
And so are **you**

A B C A

      A
Violets are **blue**
      B
Roses are red
      C
My heart is bursting
      A
With love for **you**

A A B A

> **A**
> Violets are **blue**
> **A**
> As I always **knew**
> **B**
> But the red of the roses
> **A**
> Are meant only for **you**

A A B B

> **A**
> The look in your **eye**,
> **A**
> Violet blue, doesn't **lie**
> **B**
> You've been with **another**;
> **B**
> specifically, my **brother**

As with all rhyme schemes, there are a multitude of variations on these. While a little complicated and challenging, the following variations can be very effective.

A B A A B C B B (etc.)

A
The tick of the **clock**

B
Stops dead without **you**

A
I'm a boat without a **dock**

A
A shoe without a **sock**

B
When violets turn deep **blue**

C
Spring rains raise the rose

B
The bay mourns its **dew**

B
My sock finds its **shoe**

THE BLUES

Traditional American blues songs epitomize
the most-used rhyme scheme in popular
music. Short, simple, easy to remember and
sing, the **A A A¹** scheme is used in the blues
and in other types of popular music as well.

                                         A

Sure as I stand here, those roses are **red**

                                         A

Sure as I stand here, those roses are **red**

You've done left me,   **A**^{1}

    with my flowers lyin' on your **bed**

Notice that the first two **A** lines are exactly the same. Repeating a line or phrase verbatim can be effective in a pop song in general, and in blues in particular. Notice that the third line is longer than the first two lines.

Another common variation is the **A A A**^{1} **A** blues lines, which is also taken literally:

                                           A

Sure as I stand here, those roses are **red**

                                         A

Sure as I stand here, those roses are **red**

You've done left me,   **A**^{1}

    with my flowers lyin' on your **bed**

                                           A

Yeah, sure as I stand here, those roses are **red**

LIMERICK
(A A B B A)

The limerick form in song lyrics has been around in one variation or another since the troubadours of the Middle Ages. And it's still used effectively today. It can add interest when you write the verse in an **A B C B** (or other) form and the chorus as a limerick.

                                    A
There once was a rose from **Nantucket**

                                    A
That was planted deep in a **bucket**

                        B
Carried to and **fro**

                        B
Always on the **go**

                                            A
'Twas happy 'cause no one would **pluck it**

A A B C C B

A variation on the basic limerick form
looks like this:

A
His eyes violet **blue**

A
And all that I **knew**

B
Was that I felt a sense of **wonder**

C
His hair auburn **red**

C
And what little he **said**

B
Was drowned out by the far distant **thunder**

TRIPLETS

An older, more traditional form of lyric rhyming
involves lines of three. It's good to experiment
with this form, as it often allows you to expand
your horizons musically as well as lyrically.
Working out even part of a song with an odd-
numbered rhyming scheme (as opposed to the
common groups of two or four) can add variety
to your material.

A A A B B B

      A
The daisies are bright **yellow**

      A
I'm speaking like **Othello**

      A
She's moaning like a **cello**

      B
If I'd have known **sooner**

      B
She'd be such a **crooner**

      B
I would've procured me a **tuner**

A B A B C B (C D C, etc.)

      A
I met her in a local **bar**

      B
She smelled nothing like a **rose**

      A
Smoking that big fat **cigar**

      B
And yapping on about her **woes**

      C
Yet at closin' time, she looked **good**

      B
Ain't that always how it **goes?**

The scheme possibilities are infinite, limited only by your imagination. It is important to constantly try new combinations of rhyme schemes, to mix and match styles within a song (i.e., a blues-style verse with a limerick chorus), and always avoid that classic beginning songwriter obstacle of allowing all your songs to be structured the same way.

A BRIEF HISTORY OF RHYME

Poetry originated in the ancient traditions and ceremonies of early tribal society all over the world. The art of rhyme seems to have been developed by the early Greek and Latin poets, but was more frequently used in medieval religious hymns. Later, poetry broke away from strict religious use and was developed for entertainment purposes.

The rich work of William Shakespeare (1564–1616) used rhyme for comedy and dramatic purposes. It was he who perfected the stanza, and the rhythm of his words and the beautifully haunting and lyrical sounds they create still echo in minds today.

While Shakespeare and his contemporaries used complicated rhyming schemes that would probably never find their way into a pop song, it's certainly an exciting place to look for structure ideas and lyric inspiration. The aspiring lyricists who study such work will benefit from it.

Free Verse

After centuries of strict rules regarding scheme, accent and rhyme, the American poet Walt Whitman (1819–1892) came along and shook up the poetry world. In 1855, he published a small book of poems entitled *Leaves of Grass*, which had the audacity of not rhyming. This new form was called "free verse." It was also called "trash" and "blasphemous" by many of the established critics of the day (not unlike what they called jazz, then later rock 'n' roll, then later still, rap, when those art forms first appeared on the scene).

At the turn of the century, songs coming out of Tin Pan Alley (a reference to popular songs of the time, usually written in New York) were very strict about rhymes. They were also strict about meter (the number of syllables in each line); line by line, they had to match. So there were lots of moon-spoon-June songs that, while they rhymed and were certainly good songs, were also restrictive in what they could say, and by the nature of the restrictions, tended to be corny.

By the '60s and '70s, people like Chuck Berry, John Lennon, Bob Dylan, Joni Mitchell and Mick Jagger (among many others) wrote pop songs that had "near rhymes" in them—words that didn't exactly rhyme (often referred to as "assonance"). This type of evolution happens in every art form: first rules are made, then they're perfected, then they're broken. In this instance, it allowed songwriters more freedom to express their ideas, when expressing ideas was becoming more important than merely coming up with rhymes.

In recent years, people like Adam Duritz (of Counting Crows), Michael Stipe (of R.E.M.), Alanis Morissette, and many others, are writing songs partly in free verse. Meters don't match, lines are erratically short and long, etc. A complete poetic breakdown. But this trend allows for the priority to be placed on *what's* being said and less on *how* it's being said.

The most important point is that the idea is expressed, the story is told and the feeling is conveyed. If you need to tear down the walls of strict rhyme, then do it.

Study the masters. Learn the rules. Then break them and make your own rules, thus creating your own voice.

III. The Craft of Lyric Writing

Songwriting is a craft, not just raw talent. Since you have the desire to express your thoughts in song, that already proves you have talent. Now all you have to do is get better at it.

> "I get inspired whenever I work hard," said Igor Stravinsky.

> "Genius is 1% inspiration and 99% perspiration," said Thomas Edison.

> "Shoo-be doo-be do," said Frank Sinatra, in an infamous recording session when he was so tired he couldn't remember the lyrics that someone had worked so hard to write.

The point is, you'll only get good by doing a lot of lyric writing and by consistently pushing yourself to new limits, and even then somebody might forget your words. Never be satisfied with something that's not your best. Always be working on improving a song; then quickly move on and write another. Here's a beginning songwriter's theory: every lyricist has 100 bad songs in them that they have to work out of their system before they start writing any words that are any good. Part of the reason for this is that so many songs by others have seeped into our pores that we're simply regurgitating our musical tastes. That's why it's important to write a lot. It's the only way you'll become a good lyricist.

10 TIPS TO BETTER LYRIC WRITING

1. **Save Everything.** Don't throw away any lyrics you write. Keep them in a box, a folder, a file, your sock drawer, wherever—save them even if you immediately dislike them. Later, when you're having a bout of writer's block or just want other ideas, looking through the proverbial junkyard of songs-gone-wrong can be helpful. Even if most of the lyrics are bad, later you may look back and spot one line that was really good—and then want to lift it for your new song. Or you may say, "this is all so bad, but I like the idea of the second verse..." and be able to make it into the chorus of a song that has at this point been chorusless. Or, you may just want to see how far your lyrics have come.

2. **See the Big Picture.** In those moments when you are inspired and can't write the words you hear in your head fast enough, don't get bogged down with the details—always look at the big picture. For example, if you get an idea

for the first verse, but get stuck halfway through the second verse, don't let yourself lose the feeling by staring at a blank line. Leave it blank and go on to the chorus. Only have one line for the chorus? Fine. Go on to the third verse. Write as much as you can, even if it means leaving holes in your work. When you go to look at it later, maybe finishing the second verse and a chorus will come to you easily...and meanwhile, you'll have a skeleton frame of a great song to work with.

3. **Analyze Others.** If you like the lyrics of a songwriter, don't just settle for going, "wow—those are great lyrics." Few things in our artistic life happen by accident. Good lyrics certainly don't just happen—they are formed, molded, shaped, and put in a specific order for maximum effect. If the words to a favorite song make you sad, study it—is it painting a picture? Relaying a feeling? Telling a story? How does it do that? Specifically, what line or lines? What about it makes you feel involved? What about it makes you think of something that has happened in your own life? How can you do your own version of that?

Study the work of the masters: Woody Guthrie, Ira Gershwin, Cole Porter, Lawrence Hart, Marvin Gaye, Paul Simon, Mary Chapin-

Carpenter, Tori Amos, Elvis Costello, Pete Townshend, Chrissie Hynde, Johnny Cash and the Beatles, among many others. Live, listen and learn.

4. **Analyze Yourself.** Develop the necessary ability to look at your work as objectively as possible. Often people think that everything they do stinks—or that everything they do is great. Chances are, the truth is somewhere in between. Be able to separate yourself from the story or feeling you were trying to convey, and ask yourself: Is this working? What am I trying to say? Am I saying it effectively? Am I trying to say too much? Too little? Learn to distinguish between the good and the bad in your work.

5. **Use Variety.** Search for ways to vary your music in general, and your rhyme schemes in particular. If your verse is A B A B, put your chorus in limerick form; if you have a tendency to write in first person (using "I" and "me"), take the voice of a storyteller; if you always write about yourself, your experiences and feelings, write about someone you hardly know and whose life is completely different from your own. In the bigger picture, if you always write hard rock, write a love ballad; if you write Broadway style songs, write a rock song; etc.—

if just for the exercise.

6. **Cool Off.** When you write lyrics, you'll probably love them right away. But put them away for a few days—if not a week. Later, with an objective eye, you will be in a better position to fine tune them and spot the song's weaknesses. Don't hesitate to hack at your lyrics, and also have the courage to cut a good line if it's not right for the song.

7. **Avoid Clichés.** After you've written your song and have given yourself a suitable cooling-off period, sit down with it and go over it for what's called the land mines of bad lyric writing—the cliché. If there's even one, it can ruin the song. So if there are any *cuts like a knife, spread your wings and fly* or *flies like a dove* or anything else you've heard a billion times, then make yourself say it in a different way—one that's not been heard before. Or, better still, turn the cliché inside out and twist it into something original.

8. **Expand Your Horizons.** Look to other sources for inspiration: the short stories of D.H. Lawrence or James Joyce, the poetry of Robert Frost or Gwendolyn Brooks; the writings of Maya Angelou or even Hunter S. Thompson— or even the art of Picasso or Van Gogh. Obviously you can't recreate what other great

artists from other mediums do, but it can make you think in ways that will take you outside your own individual style of lyric writing.

9. **Writer's Block Is No Excuse.** There will be times when you can't think of anything to save your life. Some people think you should wait until the creative muse visits you again, and just do nothing until that happens.

Others think there can be no excuses: you're a creator, so create. Make yourself write a song—even if what you're writing makes no sense or feels really bad. If you haven't been able to write a song in two months, then make yourself write one a day until you work yourself out of it. Actually, thumbing through this book, just looking at rhymes randomly might be all you need to get you through a dry period.

10. **Show It, Don't Say It.** It's an old saying from the theater, but it also holds true for good lyric writing. Don't say "I felt lonely when you left me" in a song—paint a picture, and show it: "I play a lot of solitaire since you've been gone."

Most of all, keep writing. And keep the faith.

A

Ability (see **Be**)

Able cable disable enable fable label sable stable table unable unstable

Abolish demolish polish tallish

Abort (see **Court**)

Abortive sportive supportive

About boy scout blow-out bout clout devout doubt eke out flout gout lout out pout roundabout route scout shout snout spout sprout stout tout trout wash-out worn-out

Above dove glove ladylove love mourning dove of shove turtle dove

Absolute (see **Cute**)

Abstract (see **Act**)

Absurd bird blackbird bluebird curd heard herd hummingbird ladybird mockingbird overheard third word yellowbird

Abuse accuse confuse cues deduce diffuse disuse duce excuse induce infuse introduce juice misuse obtuse peruse produce profuse reduce refuse reproduce seduce Syracuse use

Abyss amiss analysis armistice bliss carcass cowardice dismiss emphasis hiss hypothesis

kiss miss nemesis office prejudice Swiss
synthesis this

Academic endemic epidemic polemic systematic
(see *tick*)

Accelerate (see **Ate**)

Accept adept crept except intercept kept overslept
slept stepped swept wept

Access (see **Confess**)

Account amount count dismount fount mount
paramount tantamount

Accuse (see **Abuse**)

Ace base bass brace case chase commonplace
debase disgrace displace embrace encase erase
face grace lace mace misplace pace place race
replace space steeplechase trace unlace vase

Ache bake brake break cake fake flake forsake
headache heartache keepsake make mistake
opaque quake rake sake shake snake stake
steak take wake

Achey flaky quaky shaky snaky

Achieve believe bereave conceive disbelieve eve
grieve heave leave perceive receive relieve
reprieve retrieve sleeve weave

Achievement bereavement

Acre baker breaker dressmaker faker heartbreaker
maker matchmaker pacemaker peacemaker

Quaker shaker strikebreaker taker troublemaker undertaker watchmaker

Acrobat (see **At**)

Acrobatic (see **Attic**)

Across albatross boss cross double-cross floss gloss loss moss rhinoceros sauce toss

Act abstract attract backed compact contract distract exact fact impact intact jacked packed pact protract racked react slacked smacked snacked subtract tact tracked tract

Action abstraction attraction distraction extraction faction fraction reaction satisfaction subtraction traction transaction

Active attractive extractive inactive proactive radioactive reactive

Actor benefactor contractor detractor distracter extractor factor reactor refractor tractor

Actual contractual factual

Ad (see **Bad**)

Add (see **Bad**)

Addict conflict constrict contradict convict derelict evict flicked inflict licked predict pricked strict

Addiction affliction benediction contradiction conviction crucifixion depiction diction eviction fiction friction jurisdiction prediction restriction

Adjourn (see **Learn**)

Adjust (see **Trust**)

Admire acquire amplifier aspire attire buyer choir
conspire crier cryer desire dire dryer entire
esquire expire fire flier friar higher hire inquire
inspire justifier liar magnifier multiplier
mystifier perspire prior prophesier require
retire satisfier sire squire supplier testifier tire
transpire wire

Admirer direr enquirer hirer inquirer inspirer wirer

Admission (see **Tradition**)

Adopt copped flopped mopped opt popped stopped

Adventure denture indenture misadventure venture

Advice concise device dice entice ice lice mice nice
paradise precise price rice sacrifice spice splice
suffice thrice twice vice

Advocate (see **Ate**)

Affair (see **Air**)

Affect (see **Defect**)

Affection bisection circumspection collection
complexion connection correction defection
deflection detection direction disaffection
dissection ejection election erection
imperfection infection inflection inspection
intersection introspection objection perfection
projection protection reflection rejection
resurrection retrospection section selection

vivisection

Afford aboard accord award board bored ford harpsichord hoard lord overboard poured reward shuffleboard soared sword ward

Afraid aid arcade barricade blade blockade braid brayed brigade centigrade charade crusade degrade dismayed dissuade downgrade escapade evade fade grade grenade hayed invade laid lemonade made maid masquerade paid parade persuade played promenade raid renegade serenade shade spade stockade suede tirade trade

After grafter hereafter laughter rafter thereafter

Afternoon (see **Moon**)

Again abstain airplane arraign ascertain attain brain Cain campaign cane chain champagne cocaine complain contain crane detain disdain domain drain entertain explain feign gain grain humane hurricane hydroplane insane lane main Maine maintain mane migraine obtain ordain pain pane pertain plain plane profane propane rain refrain reign rein remain sane slain Spain sprain stain strain sustain train vain vane vein wane windowpane (see **Win**)

Against condensed fenced sensed

Age cage gage page rampage sage stage wage

Agony (see **Be**)

Agree (see **Be**)

Ailment curtailment impalement implement

Aim acclaim became blame came claim exclaim fame
flame frame game inflame lame maim name
proclaim same shame tame

Air affair anywhere aware bare bear billionaire blare
care chair compare dare debonair declare despair
disrepair elsewhere everywhere fair fare flair glare
hair hare heir impair legionnaire mare midair
millionaire nightmare pair pare pear Pierre prayer
prepare rare ready-to-wear repair scare snare
solitaire somewhere spare square stair stare
swear tear their there thoroughfare unaware
underwear unfair ware wear where

Airplane (see **Again**)

Aisle (see **Smile**)

Alarm arm charm disarm farm forearm harm

Album aquarium auditorium become bum burdensome
Christendom come cranium crematorium crumb
curriculum drum dumb emporium fee-fi-fo-fum
glum gum gymnasium hum kettledrum kingdom
martyrdom maximum meddlesome medium
millennium minimum mum museum numb
opium overcome pendulum petroleum platinum
plum premium quarrelsome radium random rum
sanitarium scum slum some strum succumb sum
swum tedium thumb Tom Thumb Tweedledum

uranium worrisome yum

Ale bail bale blackmail braille cocktail curtail exhale
fail female flail frail hail hale impale inhale jail
mail male nail pale prevail rail regale sail sale
scale shale snail stale tail they'll veil whale

Alert (see **Hurt**)

Alibi (see **Cry**)

Alien Australian Episcopalian

Alimony acrimony baloney bony crony macaroni
matrimony patrimony phony pony sanctimony
stony testimony Tony

All ball bawl brawl call crawl doll drawl enthrall fall
gall haul install mall maul Montreal nightfall
overhaul parasol pitfall protocol rainfall scrawl
shawl small snowfall sprawl stall tall thrall wall
waterfall y'all

Allege dredge edge fledge hedge ledge privilege
sacrilege sledge wedge

Alley dilly-dally rally Sally tally valley

Allow avow bough bow brow chow cow disavow
endow frau how kowtow now ow plough plow
row slough somehow sow thou vow wow

Allude (see **Feud**)

Allure (see **Cure**)

Almighty Aphrodite flighty mightily righty

Alone atone backbone baritone blown bone

chaperone clone condone cone cornerstone cyclone Dictaphone flown full-blown full-grown gramophone grindstone groan grown headstone known loan lone microphone milestone moan monotone mown overgrown overthrown own phone postpone prone saxophone sewn shown stone telephone thrown tone trombone unknown xylophone zone

Along belong bong ding-dong gong Hong Kong long Ping-Pong prong song strong throng wrong

Altar alter defaulter falter Gibraltar halter Psalter

Always hallways small ways (see *way*)

Am Amsterdam anagram Birmingham cam clam cram dam damn diaphragm gram ham jam lamb ma'am madame scram sham slam swam telegram tram yam

Amateur (see **Her**)

Amaze ablaze appraise bays blaze braze craze days daze faze gaze glaze graze haze malaise mayonnaise maze nays nowadays plays polonaise praise ways

Amble gamble ramble scramble shamble

Amen citizen den fen hen hydrogen Ken men oxygen pen regimen specimen ten then yen Zen

Among (see **Young**)

Amorous clamorous glamorous (see *us*)

Amount account count dismount fount mount paramount tantamount

Amp camp champ clamp cramp damp lamp ramp stamp vamp

Analysis catalysis dialysis paralysis (see *miss*)

Anchor banker canker flanker franker rancor ranker spanker tanker thank 'er

And band brand canned command contraband demand expand fanned grand hand land panned planned reprimand Rio Grande sand stand

Angelic relic

Angle dangle entangle jangle mangle spangle strangle tangle triangle wrangle

Anguish languish

Anniversary cursory nursery (see **Be**)

Annoy (see **Boy**)

Annual manual

Another brother mother other smother

Ant aunt can't chant decant enchant grant implant plant rant scant shan't slant transplant

Anxiety (see **Be**)

Anxiety impropriety notoriety piety propriety sobriety society variety

Any   Benny Jenny many penny

Anyone   anyone begun bun comparison done
   everyone fun Galveston gun hon Hun jettison
   none nun oblivion one outdone outrun
   overdone overrun phenomenon pun run shun
   simpleton skeleton son stun sun ton unison
   venison won

Anything   (see **Sing**)

Apart   art cart chart counterpart dart depart heart
   mart part smart start sweetheart tart upstart

Ape   cape cityscape drape escape grape landscape
   rape seascape shape tape

Apologize   (see **Lies**)

Apostle   colossal docile fossil jostle

Appalled   bald scald

Appear   (see **Near**)

Appearance   adherence clearance coherence
   disappearance incoherence interference
   perseverance

Applaud   abroad awed broad clod cod defraud
   façade fraud God guffawed Izod nod odd pod
   prod promenade quad rod roughshod shod sod
   squad trod wad

Applauding   defrauding lauding marauding plodding
   prodding

Applause   because cause clause claws gauze laws

menopause Oz pause paws Santa Claus was

Apple chapel dapple grapple scrapple

Appliance alliance compliance defiance reliance

Appreciate (see **Ate**)

Apprehensive comprehensive defensive expensive
extensive incomprehensive inexpensive
intensive offensive pensive

Approach broach coach cockroach encroach poach
reproach roach

Approve behoove disapprove disprove groove
improve move prove remove

Arbor barber harbor (see *door*)

Arcade (see **Afraid**)

Arch march parch starch

Are bar bazaar bizarre car caviar cigar Czar disbar far
guitar jar par scar sitar spar star tar

Area Bulgaria malaria

Arena Athena concertina hyena Messina subpoena
Tina

Argument (see **Bent**)

Aristocrat (see **At**)

Aristocratic (see **Attic**)

Ark aardvark arc bark dark embark hark lark mark
narc park patriarch remark shark spark stark

Arm alarm charm disarm farm forearm harm

Aroma   coma diploma sarcoma Sonoma Tacoma

Around   (see **Found**)

Arrange   change derange estrange exchange range strange

Arrow   barrow harrow marrow narrow sparrow tarot

Art   apart cart chart counterpart dart depart heart mart part smart start sweetheart tart upstart

Article   particle

Artificial   beneficial initial judicial official sacrificial superficial

Artisan   partisan

Ash   balderdash bash brash cash clash crash dash flash gnash lash mash rash rehash slash smash splash stash thrash trash

Ask   bask cask flask mask masque task

Asp   clasp gasp grasp

Ass   (see **Class**)

Assault   cobalt exalt fault halt malt salt somersault vault

Assistant   consistent distant existent inconsistent insistent persistent resistant subsistent

Asteroid   avoid alkaloid joyed Lloyd Sigmund Freud tabloid toyed void

At   acrobat aristocrat autocrat bat brat bureaucrat cat chat democrat diplomat drat fat flat gnat hat

mat pat rat rat-a-tat-tat sat scat spat stat
thermostat vat

Ate   *one syllable*:
bait crate date eight hate late mate plate rate
skate slate state straight strait trait wait weight

two syllable:
await berate debate dictate donate equate
estate frustrate irate locate narrate ornate
placate relate rotate sedate translate vacate

three syllable:
abdicate advocate aggravate agitate amputate
animate annotate arbitrate assimilate calculate
candidate captivate celebrate circulate
compensate complicate concentrate confiscate
congratulate consecrate consolidate constipate
consummate contaminate contemplate
cooperate coordinate correlate culminate
cultivate decimate decorate dedicate
demonstrate desecrate designate detonate
devastate dislocate dissipate dominate
duplicate educate elevate estimate excavate
fabricate fascinate fluctuate formulate generate
graduate gravitate habituate heavyweight
hesitate hibernate illustrate imitate implicate
incubate innovate inordinate insulate isolate
lacerate legislate levitate liberate liquidate
lubricate magistrate marinate mediate
moderate modulate motivate nominate

operate orchestrate oscillate overate overstate
overweight penetrate perpetrate populate
punctuate radiate regulate reinstate renovate
ruminate saturate second-rate separate
simulate situate speculate stimulate stipulate
suffocate tabulate terminate titillate tolerate
underrate understate underweight vacillate
validate vegetate ventilate vindicate violate

four or more syllable:
accelerate accentuate accommodate
accumulate affiliate alienate annihilate
appreciate appropriate articulate assassinate
associate collaborate commemorate
commiserate communicate conciliate
corroborate decapitate deliberate depreciate
deteriorate discriminate elaborate eliminate
emancipate emulate enunciate eradicate
evacuate evaluate evaporate excommunicate
exonerate extenuate exterminate facilitate
humiliate illuminate incapacitate incarcerate
incorporate incriminate inculcate infatuate
impersonate insinuate intimidate intoxicate
invigorate manipulate necessitate negotiate
obliterate originate participate pontificate
precipitate procrastinate reciprocate
regurgitate rehabilitate reiterate rejuvenate
resuscitate retaliate reverberate subordinate
(see *deviate*)

Athlete (see **Sweet**)

Athletic aesthetic alphabetic apathetic apologetic arithmetic cosmetic electromagnetic energetic frenetic genetic pathetic poetic sympathetic synthetic theoretic

Atlantis mantis

Atomic anatomic comic economic

Attach batch catch detach dispatch hatch latch match patch scratch snatch

Attack (see **Back**)

Attempt contempt dreamt exempt tempt unkempt

Attend (see **Friend**)

Attention abstention apprehension ascension comprehension condescension convention dissension detention dimension dissension extension intention intervention invention mention retention suspension tension

Attentive inattentive incentive inventive retentive

Attic acrobatic aristocratic aromatic autocratic bureaucratic chromatic cinematic climatic democratic dogmatic dramatic erratic fanatic melodramatic operatic pragmatic problematic static stigmatic systematic thematic traumatic

Attitude gratitude latitude platitude

Attorney journey tourney (see *be*)

Attractive active extractive inactive proactive radioactive reactive

Audition (see **Tradition**)

Aura angora aurora flora Nora sinora Torah

Autumn bottom

Avenue (see **Knew**)

Avoid alkaloid asteroid joyed Lloyd Sigmund Freud tabloid toyed void

Award (see **Lord**)

Aware (see **Air**)

Awe Arkansas awe bra caw claw draw flaw gnaw guffaw hurrah jaw law Ma macaw nah overdraw Pa paw raw saw seesaw shah slaw squaw straw thaw withdraw

Awesome blossom possum (see *some*)

Awful lawful

Awhile (see **Smile**)

Ax backs fax jacks lax max relax packs Saks sax slacks tax wax

a w e   b a l d scald

law

B

Babble dabble rabble scrabble

Baby maybe (see *be*)

Bachelor (see **Door**)

Back almanac attack black bric-a-brac Cadillac
cardiac clickety-clack egomaniac feedback hack
Hackensack haystack jack kleptomaniac knack
lack maniac pack plaque Pontiac prozac quack
rack sack shack slack snack stack tack track
whack yak zodiac

Bacon (see **Taken**)

Bad ad add Brad cad Chad clad Dad egad fad glad
grad had lad nomad pad plaid sad shad
Trinidad

Baffle raffle snaffle

Bag brag drag flag gag hag lag mag nag rag sag shag
slag snag stag swag tag wag

Bait (see **Ate**)

Balcony (see **Be**)

Bald appalled scald

Ball all bawl brawl call crawl doll drawl fall gall haul
install mall maul Montreal nightfall overhaul
parasol pitfall protocol rainfall scrawl shawl
small snowfall sprawl stall tall thrall wall
waterfall y'all

B

Ballad   invalid salad valid

Balloon   (see **Moon**)

Banana   (see **Nirvana**)

Band   and bland brand canned command contraband demand expand fanned grand hand land panned planned reprimand Rio Grande sand stand

Bandstand   grandstand handstand

Bang   boomerang clang dang fang orangutan rang sang slang sprang

Bank   blank clank crank dank drank flank frank hank outrank plank prank rank sank shrank spank stank tank thank yank

Banker   anchor canker flanker franker rancor ranker spanker tanker thank 'er

Bar   bazaar bizarre car caviar cigar Czar disbar far guitar jar par scar spar star tar

Barb   garb

Barber   arbor harbor (see *door*)

Barf   scarf snarf

Barge   charge discharge enlarge large

Bark   aardvark arc ark dark embark hark lark mark narc park patriarch remark shark spark stark

Barn   darn yarn

Barracuda Bermuda Buddha gouda

Barrage camouflage garage entourage mirage

Barrel apparel carol

Barrier carrier terrier (see *her*)

Base (see **Ace**)

Bash ash balderdash brash cash clash crash dash flash gnash lash mash rash rehash slash smash splash stash thrash trash

Basket casket gasket (see *it*, *get*)

Baste aftertaste braced chaste distaste faced freckle-faced haste hatchet-faced lambaste paste taste two-faced waist waste

Bat (see **At**)

Batch attach catch detach dispatch hatch latch match patch scratch snatch

Bath aftermath homeopath math path psychopath sociopath wrath

Battery flattery (see *be*)

Battle cattle chattel embattle prattle rattle Seattle tattle

Bay (see **Say**)

Be *one syllable:*
bee fee flea flee free gee glee he key knee me plea pea sea see she tea thee tree we wee ye

two syllable:

agree debris decree degree foresee goatee
Gumby hee-hee Marie R&D theory trustee
wintry

three syllable:

absentee agency agony amnesty ancestry
archery armory artistry bakery balcony battery
bigotry blasphemy botany bourgeoisie bravery
brevity bribery burglary Calgary calvary casualty
cavity century certainty charity chastity
chickadee chimpanzee chivalry clemency
colony comedy company courtesy crudity
cruelty custody decency deputy destiny
devotee diary dignity disagree DMZ drapery
dynasty ebony ecstasy effigy elegy embassy
employee enemy energy eulogy factory fallacy
family fantasy felony fertility fiery first-degree
flagrancy flattery fluency forgery frequency
gaiety galaxy Galilee gallantry gallery Germany
gravity guarantee harmony heresy hierarchy
history homily honesty imagery industry infamy
infancy infantry injury inquiry irony Italy ivory
jamboree jealousy jeopardy jewelry jubilee
legacy leniency levity liberty liturgy lottery
loyalty lunacy luxury melody memory mercury
mimicry ministry misery mockery modesty
mutiny mystery nominee nursery odyssey
oversee pageantry papacy parody paternity

pedantry pedigree penalty perjury Ph.D. piety
piracy pleasantry poetry poignancy policy
potpourri poverty privacy prodigy property
puberty purity quackery quality quantity rarity
recipe rectory referee refugee remedy repartee
revelry rhapsody rickety rivalry robbery
rosemary royalty salary sanctity sanity savagery
savory scarcity scenery scrutiny secrecy sesame
shadowy shivery silvery simile slavery slippery
sorcery strategy subsidy subtlety sugary
summary symmetry sympathy symphony
tapestry tendency Tennessee thievery timpani
treachery trickery trilogy trinity truancy tyranny
unity urgency victory watery witchery

four or more syllable:

ability absurdity activity actuality adversity
affinity agility ambiguity amenity animosity
anarchy anatomy anniversary anonymity
antiquity anxiety artillery astrology astronomy
atrocity audacity authenticity authority
barbarity biography biology brilliancy brutality
capacity captivity celebrity Christianity
chronology combustibility commodity
community compatibility complacency
complexity complimentary comprehensibility
conformity consistency conspiracy
contradictory criminality curiosity debauchery
deformity delivery dependency depravity

diversity diplomacy directory discovery
discrepancy divinity eccentricity economy
efficiency electricity elementary emergency
enormity epitome equality eternity expectancy
extremity facility facsimile ferocity festivity
fiddle-de-dee fidelity formality fraternity
frivolity futility generosity geography geometry
gratuity heredity hilarity hospitably hostility
humanity humility hypocrisy identity idiocy
illiteracy immodesty immunity inability
incapacity inconsistency indecency
individuality inferiority infirmary infirmity
ingenuity inhumanity insufficiency insurgency
integrity intensity legality longevity machinery
mahogany majesty maternity maturity
mediocrity minority mobility monogamy
monopoly monstrosity morality mythology
nationality nativity necessity neutrality nobility
notoriety peculiarity personality philanthropy
philosophy photography popularity
pornography posterity prosperity priority
profanity proficiency promiscuity propriety
proximity psychiatry publicity reality recovery
rudimentary satisfactory security sensibility
sensuality sentimentality serenity severity
sexuality similarity simplicity sincerity society
sophistry spontaneity stability sterility
stupidity subjectively superficiality superiority
technicality theology totality tranquillity

trriviality uniformity university utility validity
variety velocity virginity vulgarity

Beach breach each impeach leech peach preach
reach screech speech teach

Bean (see **Mean**)

Beard appeared cleared disappeared feared jeered
neared persevered smeared speared weird

Beast ceased creased deceased east feast least
pieced priest yeast

Beat athlete beet bittersweet bleat cheat compete
complete conceit concrete deceit defeat delete
deplete discreet discrete eat elite feat feet fleet
greet heat incomplete indiscreet meat meet
mistreat neat obsolete parakeet receipt repeat
retreat seat sheet sleet street suite sweet treat
wheat

Beaten cheatin' Cretan eaten Eton meetin' sweeten
unbeaten

Beautiful dutiful full (see *wool*)

Beauty cutie duty

Became (see **Aim**)

Because applause cause clause claws gauze laws
menopause Oz pause paws Santa Claus was

Become (see **Dumb**)

Bed ahead bedspread bread bred coed dead dread
fed figurehead fled flowerbed fountainhead

gingerbread head inbred lead led misled misread overfed read red riverbed said shed shred sled sped spread thoroughbred thread underfed unthread wed

Beef belief brief chief disbelief grief leaf reef relief thief

Been again aspirin begin Berlin bin chagrin chin discipline feminine fin genuine gin grin harlequin heroine in inn kin mandolin mannequin masculine moccasin origin pin saccharine shin sin skin spin thick-and-thin thin tin twin violin win within

Beer adhere appear atmosphere auctioneer bombardier career cashier cavalier chandelier cheer clear dear deer disappear ear engineer fear financier frontier gear hear hemisphere here insincere interfere jeer lavaliere leer mere mountaineer near overhear overseer peer persevere pioneer queer racketeer reappear rear revere seer severe shear sheer sincere smear sneer spear sphere stratosphere tear veneer volunteer year

Before abhor ambassador ashore auditor bachelor Baltimore boar bore chancellor chore commodore competitor conspirator contributor core corps corridor deplore dinosaur door drawer Ecuador editor emperor encore evermore explore exterior floor folklore for fore four furthermore galore governor ignore implore inferior lore matador metaphor more nevermore nor oar offshore or orator ore poor pour rapport restore roar score seashore senator señor shore Singapore snore soar sophomore sore spore store swore therefore Thor tore troubadour underscore uproar visitor whore yore your

Beg egg keg leg peg

Begin again aspirin been Berlin bin chagrin chin discipline feminine fin genuine gin grin harlequin heroine in inn kin mandolin mannequin masculine moccasin origin pin saccharine shin sin skin spin thick-and-thin thin tin twin violin win within

Beginner B.F. Skinner breadwinner dinner inner sinner skinner spinner thinner winner

Begun anyone bun comparison everyone fun Galveston gun hon Hun jettison none nun oblivion one outdone outrun overdone overrun phenomenon pun run shun simpleton skeleton son stun sun ton unison venison won

Behavior misbehavior savior

Being agreeing decreeing disagreeing farseeing fleeing foreseeing freeing guaranteeing overseeing seeing teeing unseeing

Belch squelch welch

Belief beef brief chief disbelief grief leaf relief thief

Believe achieve bereave conceive disbelieve eve grieve heave leave perceive receive relieve reprieve retrieve sleeve weave

Bell belle caramel Carmel carrousel cell clientele dell dwell excel farewell fell gel hell hotel infidel knell mademoiselle personnel sell shell smell spell tell well yell

Belly deli jelly Kelly Shelly smelly

Belong along belong bong ding-dong gong Hong Kong long Ping-Pong prong song strong throng wrong

Below (see **Blow**)

Belt Celt dealt felt heartfelt melt pelt welt

Bench clench drench French monkey wrench quench stench trench wench wrench

Bend (see **Friend**)

Beneath heath teeth underneath wreath

Beneficial artificial initial judicial official sacrificial superficial

Benevolent malevolent

Bent *one syllable:*
cent dent gent Lent lent rent sent spent tent vent went

two syllable:
accent assent cement comment convent consent content descent event ferment fluent

frequent meant percent present prevent relent
repent resent torment unbent well-meant

three syllable:
accident affluent acedent president prominent
punishment regiment represent resident
reverent sacrament sediment sentiment
settlement subsequent succulent supplement
temperament tenement testament tournament
violent wonderment

four or more syllable:
abandonment acknowledgment invent
irreverent malevolent misrepresent
predicament replenishment self-confident
diment sentiment settlement subsequent
succulent supplement temperament tenement
testament tournament violent wonderment

four or more syllable:
abandonment acknowledgment advertisement
benevolent bewilderment coincident
development disarmament embarrassment
embellishment embezzlement embodiment
encouragement enlightenment environment
establishment experiment imprisonment
incompetent ingredient intelligent intent
invent irreverent malevolent misrepresent
predicament replenishment self-confident

B

Best   arrest attest blessed breast Bucharest Budapest celeste chest congest contest crest detest digest divest dressed guessed guest infest ingest interest invest jest manifest messed molest nest pest protest request rest second-best suggest test unrest vest zest

Bet   (see **Met**)

Bethlehem   condemn gem hem phlegm requiem stem them

Better   debtor getter letter setter sweater wetter (see *her*)

Beyond   blond bond correspond dawned fond pond respond spawned vagabond wand yawned

Bible   libel tribal

Bicycle   icicle tricycle

Bid   did forbid grid hid invalid lid Madrid pyramid rid skid slid squid

Big   dig fig gig jig pig rig swig thingamajig twig wig

Bigot   spigot

Bike   hike like mike spike strike tyke

Biker   hiker piker spiker striker (see *her*)

Bill   (see **Fill**)

Bingo   dingo flamingo gringo jingo lingo (see *glow*)

Bird   absurd blackbird bluebird curd heard herd hummingbird ladybird mockingbird overheard third word yellowbird

Birth   dearth earth girth mirth worth

Biscuit   brisket (see *it*)

Bitch   bewitch ditch enrich glitch hitch pitch rich
        snitch stitch switch twitch which

Bite   (see **Night**)

Bitter   counterfeiter critter fitter fritter glitter litter
        quitter sitter transmitter twitter (see *her*)

Bizarre   are bar bazaar car caviar cigar Czar disbar far
        guitar jar par scar spar star tar

Blab   cab crab dab drab gab grab jab lab nab scab
        slab stab tab

Blade   (see **Afraid**)

Blame   acclaim aim became came claim exclaim
        fame flame frame game inflame lame maim
        name proclaim same shame tame

Blank   bank clank crank dank drank flank frank hank
        outrank plank prank rank sank shrank spank
        stank tank thank yank

Blast   aghast cast classed contrast fast flabbergast
        forecast gassed last mast outlast overcast
        passed past vast

Blatant   latent patent

Blaze   ablaze amaze appraise bays braze craze days
        daze faze gaze glaze graze haze malaise

mayonnaise maze nays nowadays plays polonaise praise ways

Blazer appraiser gazer laser maser phaser praiser razor stargazer

Bleed agreed breed centipede concede creed deed exceed feed greed heed inbreed knead lead mislead need precede proceed read recede reed secede seed speed stampede succeed Swede tweed weed

Blemish Flemish

Blend (see **Friend**)

Bless (see **Confess**)

Blind behind bind find grind hind humankind kind mastermind mind remind signed unkind unwind wind wined

Blinded evil-minded feebleminded like-minded minded narrow-minded reminded

Blink brink chink clink drink fink ink kink link mink pink rink shrink sink slink stink think wink zinc

Bliss abyss amiss analysis armistice carcass cowardice dismiss emphasis hiss hypothesis kiss miss nemesis office prejudice Swiss synthesis this

Blister assister magister mister resister sister twister (see *her*)

Blizzard gizzard lizard scissored wizard

Bloat (see **Boat**)

Blond (see **Beyond**)

Blood bud cud dud flood mud scud spud stud thud

Bloom boom broom cloakroom doom entomb flume gloom groom room tomb whom womb zoom

Blossom awesome possum (see *some*)

Blouse douse grouse house louse madhouse mouse outhouse penthouse slaughterhouse souse spouse

Blow afro although banjo beau below bestow bow buffalo bungalow calico crossbow crow depot doe domino dough embryo escrow Eskimo flow foe forgo fro gazebo gigolo glow go grow heigh-ho ho-ho hobo hoe incognito indigo Joe know long ago low Mexico mistletoe mow no oboe oh outgrow overflow overgrow overthrow owe Pinocchio pistachio plateau quo rainbow ratio roe row sew slow snow so Soho status quo stow studio tally-ho though throw tiptoe to-and-fro toe Tokyo tow tremolo undergo undertow vertigo woe yo yo-yo

Blown (see **Known**)

Blue (see **Do**)

Blues booze bruise choose cruise lose news ooze snooze whose

Bluff buff cuff duff enough fluff gruff huff muff powder puff rough scruff scuff snuff stuff tough

B

Blunder   plunder under thunder wonder

Blunt   affront bunt confront forefront front grunt
       hunt punt runt shunt stunt

Blur   (see **Her**)

Board   (see **Lord**)

Boast   coast foremost furthermost ghost host
       innermost most post roast toast whipping post

Boat   afloat antidote bloat coat connote denote dote
       float footnote gloat goat misquote moat note
       oat overcoat promote quote remote riverboat
       rote smote throat tote underwrote vote wrote

Body   embody gaudy lawdy nobody shoddy
       somebody toddy

Bold   behold blindfold centerfold cold fold foothold
       foretold gold hold household marigold mold
       old retold scold sold told uphold withhold

Bolt   colt dolt jolt revolt thunderbolt

Bomb   aplomb calm embalm Guam Mom palm
       psalm qualm

Bombard   avant-garde card chard discard disregard
       guard hard lard regard retard tarred yard

Bomber   calmer embalmer palmer (see *her*)

Bond   beyond blond correspond fond dawned pond
       respond spawned vagabond wand yawned

Bone   (see **Known**)

Book brook cook crook hook look mistook nook outlook rook shook took undertook

Boom bloom broom cloakroom doom entomb flume gloom groom room tomb whom womb zoom

Boost roost

Booth couth Duluth sleuth tooth truth uncouth youth

Booty cootie fruity snooty tutti-frutti

Booze blues bruise choose cruise lose news ooze snooze whose

Boozer accuser amuser cruiser lose 'er loser muser oozer refuser snoozer user (see *her*)

Border boarder disorder hoarder order recorder

Born adorn airborne Cape Horn Capricorn corn horn lovelorn Matterhorn morn mourn popcorn scorn stillborn sworn unicorn warn worn

Borrow morrow sorrow tomorrow

Botch blotch crotch debauch hopscotch notch Scotch watch wristwatch

Both growth loath oath overgrowth undergrowth

Bottle dottle mottle throttle waddle wattle

Bottom autumn

Bought astronaut brought caught cosmonaut fought naught ought overwrought sought taught thought wrought

B

Bounce   announce counts denounce mounts ounce pounce pronounce renounce trounce

Bound   (see **Found**)

Boundary   foundry

Bout   about boy scout blow-out clout devout doubt eke out flout gout lout out pout roundabout route scout shout snout spout sprout stout tout trout wash-out worn-out

Bow   (see **Blow**)

Bowl   (see **Control**)

Box   chickenpox equinox fox mailbox orthodox ox paradox socks stocks rocks Xerox

Boy   ahoy annoy buoy convoy corduroy coy decoy destroy employ enjoy Illinois joy ploy Roy Savoy soy toy troy viceroy

Brag   bag drag flag gag hag lag mag nag rag sag shag slag snag stag swag tag wag

Bragger   bagger carpet-bagger dagger stagger swagger tagger

Brain   (see **Chain**)

Branch   avalanche ranch

Brand   and band canned command contraband demand expand fanned grand hand land panned planned reprimand Rio Grande sand stand

Brandy Andy candy dandy handy randy sandy

Brass (see **Class**)

Brat (see **At**)

Brave behave cave concave crave engrave forgave
gave grave knave pave rave save shave slave
waive wave

Bravery savory slavery

Bread ahead bed bedspread bred coed dead dread
fed figurehead fled flowerbed fountainhead
gingerbread head inbred lead led misled
misread overfed read red riverbed said shed
shred sled sped spread thoroughbred thread
underfed unthread wed

Breadline headline deadline

Break ache bake brake cake fake flake forsake
headache heartache keepsake make mistake
opaque quake rake sake shake snake stake
steak take wake

Breakup make-up shake-up take up wake up

Breath death Macbeth

Breather either neither

Breathing seething teething

Bribe circumscribe describe jibe prescribe scribe
subscribe tribe

Brick arithmetic arsenic candlestick candlewick

Catholic chick click flick heartsick hick kick lick limerick love-sick lunatic maverick nick pick sick slick stick thick tic tick wick

Bride beside bonafide collide confide countryside decide defied died dignified divide eyed fireside guide hide hillside homicide inside lied outside override pride provide reside ride side slide snide stride subdivide subside suicide tide tried wide yuletide

Bridge abridge fridge ridge

Bright (see **Flight**)

Brilliant resilient

Bring (see **Sing**)

Broke artichoke baroque bloke choke cloak coke croak evoke folk invoke joke oak poke provoke revoke smoke soak spoke stroke toke woke yoke

Broth cloth froth moth swath wroth

Brother another mother other smother

Brought (see **Thought**)

Brown clown crown down downtown drown frown gown hand-me-down noun renown town tumble-down upside down uptown

Brunch bunch crunch hunch lunch munch punch scrunch

Brush blush crush flush gush lush mush plush rush slush thrush underbrush

Brute (see **Cute**)

Bubble double rubble stubble trouble

Buck (see **Truck**)

Bucket Nantucket (see *it*)

Buckle arbuckle chuckle honeysuckle knuckle suckle

Budge drudge fudge grudge judge misjudge nudge
     smudge

Buff (see **Bluff**)

Bug drug dug jug hug lug mug plug pug rug shrug
     slug smug snug thug tug

Bugle frugal fugal

Build chilled drilled filled guild killed rebuild willed

Builder bewilder (see *her*)

Built guilt hilt jilt kilt quilt spilt stilt tilt Vanderbilt
     wilt

Bulge divulge indulge

Bull cock-and-bull do-able full pull wool (see
     beautiful)

Bum (see **Dumb**)

Bump chump clump dump hump jump lump plump
     rump slump stump thump trump ump

Bunch brunch crunch hunch lunch munch punch
     scrunch

Bungle jungle

B

Bunny funny honey sunny

Burial aerial

Burn adjourn churn concern discern earn fern intern
          kern learn overturn return sojourn spurn stern
          taciturn turn urn yearn

Burnt learnt weren't

Burp chirp twirp usurp Wyatt Earp

Burrow borough furrow thorough

Burst cursed first nursed outburst thirst versed worst

Bury (see **Cherry**)

Bus (see **Us**)

Bush cush push

Bust (see **Trust**)

Bustle corpuscle hustle muscle mussel rustle tussle

Busy dizzy frizzy Lizzie tin lizzie tizzy

But butt cut glut gut halibut hut King Tut mutt nut
        putt rut scuttlebutt shut slut smut strut uncut

Butler scuttler subtler

Butter clutter cutter flutter gutter mutter putter
           shutter sputter strutter stutter utter

Button cuttin' glutton guttin' mutton nuthin'

Buzz abuzz buzz cause coz does fuzz was

By (see **Bye**)

Bye alibi amplify banzai barfly butterfly buy by certify clarify crucify cry defy deify deny die dignify diversify dragonfly drive-by dry dye eye firefly fly fry glorify gratify guy high horrify I identify imply July justify lie lullaby modify my mystify notify passerby pie pry qualify rely rye satisfy sci-fi shy sigh signify simplify sky sly specify spry spy terrify testify thigh tie try underlie verify why

buzz
cause
burn
turn
bunny   butter
cutter
sunny

C

C

Cab blab crab dab drab gab grab jab lab nab scab slab stab tab

Cable (see **Able**)

Cad (see **Bad**)

Cage age gage page rampage sage stage wage

Calf carafe epitaph giraffe graph paragraph phonograph photograph polygraph riffraff staff telegraph

Call all ball bawl brawl crawl doll drawl fall gall haul install mall maul Montreal nightfall overhaul parasol pitfall protocol rainfall scrawl shawl small snowfall sprawl stall tall thrall wall waterfall y'all

Calm aplomb bomb CD-ROM embalm Guam Mom palm psalm qualm

Calmer bomber embalmer palmer

Calorie gallery Mallory salary

Camp amp champ clamp cramp damp lamp ramp stamp vamp

Can ban can-can Dan fan Iran man Nan plan ran Tehran

Can't ant aunt chant decant enchant grant implant plant rant scant shan't slant transplant

Canal chorale gal morale pal shall

Canary (see **Cherry**)

Candidate (see **Ate**)

Candle dandle handle sandal scandal vandal

Candy Andy brandy dandy handy randy sandy

Cap chap clap flap gap handicap lap map mishap nap rap sap scrap slap snap strap tap trap wrap zap

Cape ape cityscape drape escape grape landscape rape seascape shape tape

Captive adaptive (see *active*)

Captivity (see **Be**)

Capture rapture recapture (see *your*)

Car are bar bazaar bizarre caviar cigar czar disbar far guitar jar par scar spar star tar

Carat carrot parrot

Card avant-garde bombard card discard disregard guard hard lard regard retard tarred yard

Care affair air anywhere aware bare bear billionaire blare chair compare dare debonair declare despair disrepair elsewhere everywhere fair fare flair glare hair hare heir impair legionnaire mare midair millionaire nightmare pair pare pear Pierre prayer prepare rare ready-to-wear repair scare snare solitaire somewhere spare square stair stare swear tear their there

C

    thoroughfare unaware underwear unfair ware wear where

Career (see **Near**)

Cargo argot embargo Fargo largo

Carol apparel barrel

Carp harp sharp

Carriage disparage marriage miscarriage

Carry hari-kari marry miscarry parry vary (see *cherry*)

Cart apart art chart counterpart dart depart heart mart part smart start sweetheart tart upstart

Cartoon (see **Moon**)

Carve starve

Case (see **Ace**)

Cash ash balderdash bash brash clash crash dash flash gnash rash rehash slash smash splash stash thrash trash

Casino andantino bambino Filipino keno Reno

Cask ask bask flask mask masque task

Casket basket gasket (see *it*, *get*)

Cast aghast blast classed contrast fast flabbergast forecast gassed last mast outlast overcast passed past vast

Castle tassel vassal wrassle

Casualty (see **Be**)

Cat (see **At**)

Catch attach batch detach dispatch hatch latch
    match patch scratch snatch

Catch etch fetch kvetch retch sketch stretch wretch

Catcher dispatcher scratcher snatcher

Catholic (see **Brick**)

Cattle battle chattel embattle prattle rattle Seattle
    tattle

Caught astronaut bought brought cosmonaut fought
    naught ought overwrought sought taught
    thought wrought

Cause applause because clause claws gauze laws
    menopause Oz pause paws Santa Claus was

Cave behave brave concave crave engrave forgave
    gave grave knave pave rave save shave slave
    waive wave

Cavern tavern (see *burn*)

Caviar are bar bazaar bizarre car cigar czar disbar far
    guitar jar par scar spar star tar

Cavity depravity gravity

Celebrate (see **Ate**)

Cell bell belle caramel Carmel carrousel clientele
    dell dwell excel farewell fell gel hell hotel
    infidel knell mademoiselle personnel sell shell
    smell spell swell tell well yell

Cellar dweller feller fortuneteller interstellar

propeller Rockefeller seller smeller speller
stellar sweller teller

Cello bellow fellow hello mellow Othello yellow

Censor censer condenser denser dispenser fencer
Spencer

Cent (see **Bent**)

Center dissenter enter experimenter frequenter
inventor mentor presenter preventer renter
tormentor

Chain abstain again airplane arraign ascertain attain
brain Cain campaign cane champagne cocaine
complain contain crane detain disdain domain
drain entertain explain feign gain grain
humane hurricane hydroplane insane lane
main Maine maintain mane migraine obtain
ordain pain pane pertain plain plane profane
propane rain refrain reign rein remain sane
slain Spain sprain stain strain sustain train
vain vane vein wane windowpane

Chair (see **Air**)

Champ amp camp clamp cramp damp lamp ramp
stamp vamp

Champagne (see **Chain**)

Chance advance ants circumstance dance enhance
extravagance finance France glance lance pants
prance romance stance trance

Change arrange derange estrange exchange range
strange

Channel flannel panel

Chapel apple dapple grapple scrapple

Charade (see **Afraid**)

Charge barge discharge enlarge large

Charm arm alarm disarm farm forearm harm

Chaste baste aftertaste braced distaste faced freckle-
      faced haste hatchet-faced lambaste paste taste
      waist waste

Chat (see **At**)

Chauffeur gopher loafer (see *her*)

Cheap barkeep cheep creep deep heap keep leap
      peep reap seep sheep sleep steep sweep weep

Cheat athlete beat beet bittersweet bleat compete
      complete conceit concrete deceit defeat delete
      deplete discreet discrete eat elite feat feet fleet
      greet heat incomplete indiscreet meat meet
      mistreat neat obsolete parakeet receipt repeat
      retreat seat sheet sleet street suite sweet treat
      wheat

Cheated bleated competed completed conceited
      defeated deleted depleted excreted greeted
      heated maltreated pleated repeated retreated
      seated secreted sleeted treated

Check Czech deck fleck heck neck peck Quebec speck
      trek wreck

Cheer adhere appear atmosphere auctioneer beer

C

bombardier career cashier cavalier chandelier clear dear deer disappear ear engineer fear financier frontier gear hear hemisphere here insincere interfere jeer lavaliere leer mere mountaineer near overhear overseer peer persevere pioneer queer racketeer reappear rear revere seer severe shear sheer sincere smear sneer spear sphere stratosphere tear veneer volunteer year

Cheese (see **Ease**)

Chef clef deaf

Cherry adversary airy arbitrary beneficiary berry bury canary capillary cautionary commentary culinary customary dairy dictionary dietary dignitary disciplinary discretionary evolutionary extraordinary fairy February ferry functionary hairy hereditary honorary imaginary incendiary intermediary January Jerry legendary legionary literary luminary Mary mercenary military momentary monetary mortuary nary necessary obituary ordinary Perry planetary prairie proprietary pulmonary reactionary revolutionary sanctuary sanitary scary secretary seminary sherry solitary stationary temporary Terry Tipperary very visionary vocabulary voluntary wary

Chess (see **Confess**)

Chest arrest attest best blessed breast Bucharest

Budapest celeste congest contest crest detest digest divest dressed guessed guest infest ingest interest invest jest manifest messed molest nest pest protest request rest second-best suggest test unrest vest zest

C

Chew (see **Knew**)

Chick (see **Brick**)

Chicken quicken sicken stricken thicken (see in)

Chief beef belief brief disbelief grief leaf relief thief

Child dialed mild piled smiled wild

Chill bill daffodil distill drill frill fulfill gill grill hill ill imbecile instill kill mill nil quill shrill sill skill spill still swill thrill till trill until whippoorwill will windmill windowsill

Chilling (see **Willing**)

Chime climb crime dime I'm lime mime pantomime prime rhyme slime summertime thyme time

Chin (see **Been**)

Chip (see **Trip**)

Chirp blurp burp chirp twirp usurp Wyatt Earp

Chivalry delivery livery shivery slivery

Choice invoice rejoice voice

Choir (see **Fire**)

Choke artichoke baroque bloke broke cloak coke croak evoke folk invoke joke oak poke provoke

Prefixes: pre, re, in, con, de, mis

revoke smoke soak spoke stroke toke woke yoke

Choose blues booze bruise cruise lose news ooze snooze whose

Chop (see **Drop**)

Chopper (see **Proper**)

Chore (see **Door**)

Chorus Brontosaurus sonorous Taurus thesaurus (see *us*)

Chose arose close compose decompose depose disclose dispose doze enclose expose foreclose froze goes hose impose indispose interpose knows nose owes pose predispose presuppose prose recompose rose suppose those toes transpose woes

Christ diced feist heist iced zeitgeist

Christen glisten listen

Christianity (see **Be**)

Christmas isthmus (see *us*)

Chrome chromosome comb dome foam gnome home honeycomb metronome Nome poem roam Rome tome

Chuckle arbuckle buckle honeysuckle knuckle suckle

Chunk bunk chunk cyberpunk drunk dunk flunk funk hunk junk monk plunk punk shrunk skunk slunk spunk stunk sunk trunk

Church besmirch birch lurch perch research search smirch

Cigar are bar bazaar bizarre car caviar czar disbar far guitar jar par scar spar star tar

Cinch flinch inch lynch pinch

Cinematic (see **Attic**)

Citizen amen den fen hen hydrogen Ken men oxygen pen regimen specimen ten then yen zen

City committee ditty gritty kitty pity pretty self-pity witty

Civil drivel shrivel snivel swivel

Class alas amass ass bass brass crass gas glass grass harass hourglass lass looking-glass mass morass mustache overpass pass sass sassafras surpass

Claw Arkansas awe bra caw claw draw flaw gnaw guffaw hurrah jaw law Ma macaw nah overdraw Pa paw raw saw seesaw shah slaw squaw straw thaw withdraw

Clean bean between caffeine canteen chlorine codeine Colleen convene cuisine dean demean evergreen Florentine foreseen gasoline Gene green guillotine Halloween in-between intervene kerosene lean lien machine marine mean mezzanine Nazarene nectarine nicotine obscene preen quarantine queen ravine routine sardine scene seen serene spleen submarine

C

tambourine tangerine teen thirteen (etc.)
Vaseline velveteen wintergreen wolverine

Cleanse　bends dens lens mends sends tends

Clearance　adherence appearance coherence
disappearance incoherence interference
perseverance

Clerk　handiwork irk jerk Kirk lurk murk overwork perk
quirk shirk smirk Turk work

Clever　endeavor ever forever however lever never
sever whatever whenever wherever whoever

Client　compliant defiant giant reliant self-reliant

Cliff　handkerchief if sniff stiff tiff whiff

Climate　primate (see *it, ate*)

Climatic　(see **Attic**)

Climb　chime crime dime I'm lime mime pantomime
prime rhyme slime summertime thyme time

Clock　Bangkok beanstalk boondock cock cornstalk
crock deadlock defrock dock flintlock flock frock
gawk gridlock hawk hock J.S. Bach jock knock
Little Rock livestock lock mock Mohawk
padlock peacock rock shock sidewalk small talk
smock sock squawk stalk stock talk tomahawk
unlock walk wok

Clog　analog bog catalog cog fog demagogue
dialogue dog epilogue flog frog grog hog jog
log monologue synagogue travelogue

Close　adios bellicose comatose diagnose dose

engross grandiose gross morose nose overdose varicose verbose

Close arose chose compose decompose depose disclose dispose doze enclose expose foreclose froze goes hose impose indispose interpose knows nose owes pose predispose presuppose prose recompose rose suppose those toes transpose woes

Cloth broth froth moth swath wroth

Cloud allowed aloud crowd enshroud loud plowed proud shroud thundercloud

Cloudy cum laude dowdy howdy rowdy

Clover Dover drover moreover over rover (see *her*)

Clown brown crown down downtown drown frown gown hand-me-down noun renown town tumble-down upside down uptown

Club Beelzebub bub cub grub hub hubbub pub rub rub-a-dub-dub scrub shrub snub stub sub tub

Clue (see **Do**)

Clutch crutch Dutch hutch inasmuch much retouch such touch

Coach approach broach cockroach encroach poach reproach roach

Coal (see **Control**)

Coarse course divorce endorse force horse Norse reinforce remorse resource source

Coast boast foremost furthermost ghost host
innermost most post roast toast whipping post

Coastal postal

Coat (see **Boat**)

Coax cholks folks hoax jokes polks smokes spokes
yokes

Cockroach approach broach coach encroach poach
reproach roach

Code (see **Road**)

Coffee toffee (see *me*)

Coffin coughin' often soften

Coherent adherent incoherent inherent perseverant

Coil broil foil loyal oil recoil royal spoil toil turmoil

Coin Des Moines groin join loin purloin sirloin
tenderloin

Coincidence (see **Fence**)

Cold behold blindfold bold centerfold fold foothold
foretold gold hold household marigold mold
old retold scold sold told uphold withhold

Collapse caps craps elapse flaps lapse maps naps
perhaps saps traps wraps

Collar bawler brawler call 'er caller choler crawler
dollar hauler mauler scrawler smaller squalor
taller

Collect (see **Defect**)

Collection (see **Affection**)

College acknowledge knowledge (see *ledge*)

Collision (see **Vision**)

Color discolor duller sculler Technicolor

Coma aroma diploma sarcoma Sonoma Tacoma

Comb chrome chromosome dome foam gnome
home honeycomb metronome Nome poem
roam Rome tome

Come album aquarium auditorium become bum
burdensome Christendom cranium
crematorium crumb curriculum drum dumb
emporium fee-fi-fo-fum glum gum gymnasium
hum kettledrum kingdom martyrdom
maximum meddlesome medium millennium
minimum mum museum numb opium
overcome pendulum petroleum platinum plum
premium quarrelsome radium random rum
sanitarium scum slum some strum succumb
sum swum tedium thumb Tom Thumb
Tweedledum uranium worrisome yum

Comedy (see **Be**)

Comfort (see **Court**)

Comic atomic anatomic economic

Commercial controversial

Commune attune dune immune impugn
inopportune June tune (see *moon*)

C

Communicate (see **Ate**)

Company (see **Be**)

Complain (see **Chain**)

Complete athlete beat beet bittersweet bleat cheat
complete conceit concrete deceit defeat delete
deplete discreet discrete eat elite feat feet fleet
greet heat incomplete indiscreet meat meet
mistreat neat obsolete parakeet receipt repeat
retreat seat sheet sleet street suite sweet treat
wheat

Complex decks duplex ex flex necks pecks reflex
Rolidex specs Tex unisex

Complexion (see **Affection**)

Complicate (see **Ate**)

Compliment (see **Cent**)

Compute (see **Cute**)

Computer (see **Suitor**)

Con Amazon autobahn Babylon bonbon Bonn brawn
chiffon dawn drawn echelon fawn gone lawn
neon on pawn pentagon silicon swan
undergone upon wan woebegone wonton yawn

Concentrate (see **Ate**)

Concern adjourn burn churn discern earn fern intern
kern learn overturn return sojourn spurn stern
taciturn turn urn yearn

Concert (see **Hurt**)

Concrete (see **Sweet**)

Condemn Bethlehem gem hem phlegm requiem
   stem them

Condition acquisition addition admission ambition
   ammunition attrition audition coalition
   commission competition composition
   definition demolition deposition disposition
   edition electrician emission exhibition
   expedition exposition extradition fission
   ignition imposition inhibition inquisition
   intermission intuition magician mathematician
   mission musician nutrition omission
   opposition partition permission petition
   physician politician position prohibition
   proposition recognition rendition repetition
   requisition statistician submission superstition
   technician tradition transmission transposition
   transition tuition (see *in*)

Conduct abduct construct deduct instruct obstruct
   plucked viaduct

Confess access address baroness bashfulness
   bitterness bless caress chess cleverness
   cloudiness compress craziness deadliness
   depress digress distress dizziness dress duress
   eagerness easiness eeriness emptiness excess
   express finesse foolishness ghostliness guess
   happiness haziness homelessness idleness
   impress joyfulness joylessness laziness less

C

limitless Loch Ness lustfulness mess
nervousness obsess openness oppress
outrageousness penniless playfulness possess
press profess progress queasiness recess
regress repossess repress rockiness seediness
shallowness silkiness sleaziness sleepiness
sneakiness SOS spaciousness spitefulness
stress success suppress thoughtfulness
transgress uselessness viciousness willingness
wishfulness worldliness yes youthfulness

Confession aggression compression concession
depression digression discretion expression
impression indiscretion obsession oppression
possession procession profession progression
recession regression repression secession
session succession suppression transgression

Confetti jetty machete petty spaghetti sweaty

Confidential credential deferential differential
essential existential influential nonessential
potential preferential presidential providential
prudential quintessential residential
sequential torrential

Conflict addict constrict contradict convict derelict
evict flicked inflict licked predict pricked strict

Conform chloroform conform deform form inform
norm perform rainstorm reform snowstorm
storm swarm transform uniform warm

Confuse abuse accuse cues deduce diffuse disuse

duce excuse induce infuse introduce juice
misuse obtuse peruse produce profuse reduce
refuse reproduce seduce Syracuse use

Conquer conker honker

Consist (see **Exist**)

Contain (see **Chain**)

Contribution (see *revolution*)

Control bowl buttonhole cajole casserole coal dole
droll enroll goal hole loophole Maypole mole
Old King Cole oriole parole patrol pole poll
porthole role roll scroll tadpole toll troll whole

Convention (see **Tension**)

Converge (see **Verge**)

Convince hints mints prince rinse since wince

Cook book brook crook hook look mistook nook
outlook rook shook took undertook

Cool April fool drool fool ghoul Liverpool overrule
pool rule school spool stool tool whirlpool

Cop chop crop drop eavesdrop flop hop lollipop
mop plop pop prop raindrop shop stop swap
tip-top whop

Cope antelope cantaloupe dope elope envelope
grope gyroscope hope horoscope kaleidoscope
microscope mope pope rope scope slope soap
stethoscope telescope

Core (see **Door**)

Cork fork New York pork torque stork uncork

Corn adorn airborne born Cape Horn Capricorn horn
     lovelorn Matterhorn morn mourn popcorn
     scorn stillborn sworn unicorn warn worn

Corny horny thorny

Correct (see **Defect**)

Corrupt abrupt cupped disrupt erupt interrupt
     supped

Cost bossed crossed exhaust flossed frost holocaust
     lost Pentecost tossed

Cottage wattage

Cotton begotten gotten forgotten rotten

Couch crouch grouch ouch pouch slouch vouch

Cough off scoff trough

Could brotherhood fatherhood firewood good
     Hollywood hood likelihood livelihood
     misunderstood motherhood neighborhood
     should sisterhood stood understood withstood
     womanhood wood would

Count account amount dismount fount mount
     paramount tantamount

Couple supple

Course coarse divorce endorse force horse Norse
     reinforce remorse resource source

Court abort assort cavort comfort contort davenport

deport distort escort exhort export extort fort import passport port quart report resort retort short snort sort sport support thwart tort transport wart

Cousin buzzin' cussin' dozen fusin' musin'

Cove by Jove clove dove drove grove rove

Cover discover hover lover recover rediscover shover undercover (see *her*)

Cow allow avow bough bow brow chow disavow endow frau how kowtow now ow plough plow row slough somehow sow thou vow wow

Coy (see **Boy**)

Crab blab cab dab drab gab grab jab lab nab scab slab stab tab

Crabby abbey cabby flabby grabby scabby shabby tabby

Craft draft draught graft overdraft witchcraft

Cranky bank blank clank crank dank drank flank frank hank outrank plank prank rank sank shrank spank stank tank thank yank

Cranky hanky lanky Yankee

Craze ablaze amaze appraise bays braze days daze faze gaze glaze graze haze malaise mayonnaise maze nays nowadays plays polonaise praise ways

Crazy daisy hazy lazy

Cream   beam deem dream esteem extreme gleam ream regime scheme scream seam seen steam stream supreme team teem

Creative (see **Native**)

Creature bleacher feature preacher screecher teacher

Credit accredit discredit edit (see it)

Crept accept adept except intercept kept overslept slept stepped swept wept

Crew (see **Do**)

Cricket picket thicket ticket wicket (see *it*)

Crime chime climb dime I'm lime mime pantomime prime rhyme slime summertime thyme time

Cringe binge fringe hinge infringe singe

Crisp lisp wisp

Critic analytic arthritic hypocritic paralytic parasitic Semitic (see *tick*)

Critical analytical political

Crock (see **Clock**)

Crocodile (see **Smile**)

Cross across albatross boss double-cross floss gloss loss moss rhinoceros sauce toss

Crow afro although banjo beau below bestow blow bow buffalo bungalow calico crossbow depot doe domino dough embryo escrow Eskimo flow foe forgo fro gazebo gigolo glow go grow heigh-ho ho-ho hobo hoe incognito indigo Joe know long ago low Mexico mistletoe mow no oboe oh outgrow overflow overgrow overthrow owe Pinocchio pistachio plateau quo rainbow ratio roe row sew slow snow so Soho status quo stow studio tally-ho though throw tiptoe to-and-fro toe Tokyo tow tremolo undergo undertow vertigo woe yo yo-yo

Crowd allowed aloud cloud enshroud loud plowed proud shroud thundercloud

Crown (see **Clown**)

Crucifix acrobatics bics fiddlesticks fix kicks licks mathematics mix nix picks politics six sticks Styx ticks transfix tricks wicks

Crucifixion addiction affliction benediction contradiction conviction depiction diction eviction fiction friction jurisdiction prediction restriction

Crude brood clued conclude dude exclude food glued include intrude misconstrued mood preclude prude rude seclude shrewd wooed

Cruel duel fuel jewel

Crumb (see **Dumb**)

Crumble bumble fumble grumble humble jumble mumble rumble stumble tumble

C

Crusade (see **Afraid**)

Crush blush brush flush gush lush mush plush rush
slush thrush underbrush

Crutch clutch Dutch hutch inasmuch much retouch
such touch

Cry alibi amplify banzai barfly butterfly buy by bye
certify clarify crucify defy deify deny die dignify
diversify dragonfly drive-by dry dye eye firefly
fly fry glorify gratify guy high horrify I identify
imply July justify lie lullaby modify my mystify
notify passerby pie pry qualify rely rye satisfy
sci-fi shy sigh signify simplify sky sly specify
spry spy terrify testify thigh tie try underlie
verify why

Crypt chipped dipped equipped manuscript script
sipped transcript whipped zipped

Crystal pistol

Cuba scuba tuba

Cube boob rube tube

Cucumber cumber encumber lumber number
slumber umber

Cuddle fuddle huddle muddle puddle

Cue (see **Knew**)

Cuff (see **Bluff**)

Culture agriculture vulture

Cup buttercup fed up hard-up pick-up pup sup up

Cupid stupid

Curb blurb 'burb disturb herb perturb Serb suburb
superb verb

Cure allure armature assure brochure caricature
cocksure demure endure ensure expenditure
forfeiture immature impure insecure insure
liqueur literature lure manicure mature
miniature obscure overture pedicure premature
pure reassure secure signature sure tablature
temperature your

Curious (see **Us**)

Curl earl girl hurl pearl swirl twirl whirl

Curly burly curly girlie pearly squirrelly surly swirly

Curse adverse converse disburse disperse diverse
hearse immerse intersperse inverse nurse
purse rehearse reverse terse transverse traverse
universe verse worse

Curt (see **Hurt**)

Curve conserve deserve nerve observe preserve
reserve serve swerve

Cuss (see **Us**)

Custody (see **Be**)

Cut but butt glut gut halibut hut King Tut mutt nut
putt rut scuttlebutt shut slut smut strut uncut

Cute absolute acute astute attribute beaut boot
brute Butte chute commute compute
constitute coot destitute dilute dispute
disrepute dissolute electrocute enroute
execute flute fruit hoot loot lute minute moot
mute newt parachute persecute pollute
prosecute prostitute pursuit recruit refute
repute resolute root route scoot shoot snoot
substitute suit toot transmute uproot

d a r t

part

d a s h

d a n d e l i o n

cryin'

dash

d a i s y

crazy

D

D

Dad (see **Mad**)

Daddy baddy caddie laddie paddy sugar daddy

Dagger carpetbagger stagger swagger

Daily Bailey gaily Israeli ukulele

Dairy (see **Cherry**)

Daisy crazy hazy lazy

Damn (see **Am**)

Dance advance ants chance circumstance enhance
extravagance finance France glance lance pants
prance romance stance trance

Dandelion buyin' cryin' denyin' dyin' lion lyin' Orion
Ryan sighin' tryin' Zion (see *in*)

Dang bang boomerang clang fang orangutan rang
sang slang sprang

Dangerous (see **Us**)

Dare (see **Air**)

Dark aardvark arc ark bark embark hark lark mark
narc park patriarch remark shark spark stark

Dart apart art cart chart counterpart depart heart
mart part smart start sweetheart tart upstart

Dash ash balderdash bash brash cash clash crash
flash gnash rash rehash slash smash splash
stash thrash trash

Prefixes: pre, re, in, con, de, mis

Date (see **Ate**)

Daughter blotter hotter otter plotter slaughter
spotter squatter trotter water

Dawn Amazon Babylon begone bonbon Bonn brawn
chiffon con Don drawn fawn gone hexagon John
lawn lexicon octagon on Oregon pawn
pentagon silicon undergone upon withdrawn
wanton yawn

Day array bay betray bluejay bouquet bray clay decay
delay disarray dismay display eh? essay exposé
fray gay gray hay hey holiday hooray José Kay
lay matinee may moiré naysay negligée obey
pay play portray protégé ray résumé ricochet
risqué rosé say slay sleigh soufflé stay stray
sway they toupee way weigh x-ray

Dead ahead bed bedspread bread bred coed dread
fed figurehead fled flowerbed fountainhead
gingerbread head inbred lead led misled
misread overfed read red riverbed said shed
shred sled sped spread thoroughbred thread
underfed unthread wed

Deaf chef clef

Deal (see **Feel**)

Dealer congealer feeler healer reeler sealer squealer
stealer wheeler

Dear (see **Near**)

Death breath Macbeth

Debate (see **Ate**)

Debt   alphabet bayonet bet brunette cabinet cadet cigarette clarinet cornet corvette duet epithet etiquette forget fret gazette get jet Joliet Juliet let luncheonette marionette met net omelet pet quartet regret roulette set silhouette Somerset sunset sweat threat Tibet toilette upset vet 'vette violet wet yet

Decay (see **Say**)

Decease   cease crease decrease fleece geese grease Greece increase lease mantelpiece masterpiece peace piece police release

Decent   indecent recent

Deception   conception contraception exception inception perception preconception reception self-deception

Decision (see **Vision**)

Deck   check Czech fleck heck neck peck Quebec speck trek wreck

Decline (see **Fine**)

Decoy (see **Boy**)

Dedicate (see **Ate**)

Deduct   abduct conduct construct instruct obstruct plucked viaduct

Deep   barkeep cheep creep heap keep leap peep reap seep sheep sleep steep sweep weep

Prefixes: pre, re, in, con, de, mis

D

Defeat   athlete beat beet bittersweet bleat cheat compete complete conceit concrete deceit delete deplete discreet discrete eat elite feat feet fleet greet heat incomplete indiscreet meat meet mistreat neat obsolete parakeet receipt repeat retreat seat sheet sleet street suite sweet treat wheat

Defect   affect architect bisect checked collect connect correct deflect dialect direct disinfect dissect effect eject erect expect genuflect incorrect inject neglect object pecked perfect project prospect protect recollect reflect reject respect select subject suspect wrecked

Defendant   ascendant attendant dependent descendant independent pendant superintendent transcendent

Defender   (see **Tender**)

Defense   (see **Fence**)

Defensive   apprehensive comprehensive expensive extensive incomprehensive inexpensive intensive offensive pensive

Defer   amateur blur chauffeur concur confer connoisseur demur deter fur her incur infer Jennifer myrrh occur per prefer purr recur sir slur spur stir transfer voyageur were whir

Defiance   alliance appliance compliance reliance

Degree   (see **Be**)

Delay (see **Say**)

Deli belly jelly Kelly Shelly smelly

Delicious (see **Vicious**)

Delight (see **Flight**)

Deliver giver liver quiver river shiver sliver (see *her*)

Delivery chivalry livery shivery slivery quivery

Demand and band brand canned command contraband expand fanned grand hand land panned planned reprimand Rio Grande sand stand

Demo memo

Demolish (See **Abolish**)

Denial dial retrial self-denial trial viol (see *vile*)

Dent (see **Bent**)

Dental (see **Gentle**)

Dentist apprenticed

Deny (see **Cry**)

Depart apart art cart chart counterpart dart heart mart part smart start sweetheart tart upstart

Depot (see **Blow**)

Depression aggression compression concession confession digression discretion expression impression indiscretion obsession oppression possession procession profession progression recession regression repression secession session succession suppression transgression

D

Deputy (see **Be**)

Describe bribe circumscribe jibe prescribe scribe
subscribe tribe

Deserve conserve curve nerve observe preserve
reserve serve swerve

Desire acquire admire amplifier aspire attire buyer
choir conspire crier cryer dire drier dryer entire
esquire expire fire flier friar higher hire inquire
inspire justifier liar magnifier multiplier
mystifier perspire prior prophesier require
retire satisfier sire squire supplier testifier tire
transpire wire

Desk burlesque grotesque picturesque

Desperado bravado Colorado El Dorado Laredo
Mikado tornado

Dessert alert avert blurt concert convert curt desert
dirt divert exert expert extrovert flirt hurt insert
introvert invert pervert shirt skirt squirt subvert
yogurt

Destroy (see **Boy**)

Deviate abbreviate alleviate (see *ate*)

Devil bedevil bevel dishevel level revel

Diagnosis narcosis neurosis prognosis psychosis

Dial denial retrial self-denial trial viol (see *vile*)

Diary fiery priory Valkyrie wiry

Dice advice concise device entice ice lice mice nice

paradise precise price rice sacrifice spice splice suffice thrice twice vice

Dictate (see **Ate**)

D

Did bid forbid grid hid invalid lid Madrid pyramid rid skid slid squid

Die (see **Cry**)

Died beside bonafide bride collide confide countryside decide defied died dignified divide eyed fireside guide hide hillside homicide inside lied outside override pride provide reside ride side slide snide stride subdivide subside suicide tide tried wide yuletide

Diet riot quiet (see *it*)

Differ sniffer stiffer (see *her*)

Difference (see **Fence**)

Dig big dig fig gig jig pig renege rig swig twig wig

Digest (see **Best**)

Digit fidget midget widget

Dignify signify (see *cry*)

Dime chime climb crime I'm lime mime pantomime prime rhyme slime summertime thyme time

Dimension (see **Tension**)

Dimple pimple simple

Dine (see **Fine**)

Diner cosigner designer eyeliner finer liner miner
minor refiner shiner signer

Dinner B.F. Skinner beginner breadwinner inner
sinner skinner spinner thinner

Dinosaur (see **Door**)

Dip (see **Trip**)

Diploma aroma coma sarcoma Sonoma Tacoma

Direct (see **Defect**)

Direction (see **Affection**)

Director collector connector detector deflector
injector inspector nectar objector projector
prospector protector reflector selector vector
(see *her*)

Directory rectory

Dirt (see **Hurt**)

Dirty flirty thirty

Disco Cisco Crisco San Francisco

Discuss (see **Us**)

Disease aborigines appease bees breeze cheese
ease expertise freeze Hercules keys knees peas
pleas please sees seize Siamese sleaze squeeze
tease trapeze 'zzzs

Disgrace ace base bass brace case chase commonplace debase displace embrace encase erase
face grace lace mace misplace pace place race

D

replace space steeplechase trace unlace vase

Disgust adjust August bust crust distrust encrust entrust gust just lust mistrust must robust rust thrust trust unjust

Dish devilish fish gibberish impoverish squish swish wish

Dismay (see **Say**)

Distance assistance consistence existence insistence persistence resistance subsistence

Distant assistant consistent existent inconsistent insistent persistent resistant subsistent

Distaste baste aftertaste braced chaste faced freckle-faced haste hatchet-faced paste taste waist waste

Distinction extinction

Distort (see **Court**)

Distortion abortion contortion extortion portion proportion

Ditch bewitch bitch ditch enrich glitch hitch pitch rich snitch stitch switch twitch which

Divinity (see **Be**)

Divorce coarse course endorse force horse Norse reinforce remorse resource source

Dizzy busy frizzy Lizzie tin lizzie tizzy

Do accrue ado bamboo blew blue boo boohoo brew

D

caribou cashew clue construe coo coup crew cuckoo drew flew flue glue gnu goo grew Hindu hitherto hullabaloo igloo impromptu into issue Kalamazoo kangaroo kazoo kickapoo misconstrue moo outdo overdo overthrew peekaboo Peru poo rendezvous screw shampoo shoe shoo shrew Sioux slew slue stew taboo tattoo threw through tissue to too true two undo voodoo wahoo well-to-do who withdrew woo yahoo zoo Zulu (see *you*)

Dock (see **Clock**)

Dodge dislodge hodgepodge lodge

Does abuzz buzz cause coz fuzz was

Dog analog bog catalog clog cog fog demagogue dialogue epilogue flog frog grog hog jog log monologue synagogue travelogue underdog

Dole (see **Control**)

Dollar bawler brawler call 'er caller choler collar crawler hauler mauler scrawler smaller squalor taller

Dolly collie finale folly golly jolly melancholy Molly Polly tamale trolley volley

Donate (see **Ate**)

Done anyone begun bun comparison everyone fun Galveston gun hon Hun jettison none nun oblivion one outdone outrun overdone overrun phenomenon pun run shun simpleton skeleton son stun sun ton unison venison won

Doom bloom boom broom cloakroom entomb flume gloom groom room tomb whom womb zoom

D

Door abhor ambassador ashore auditor bachelor Baltimore before boar bore chancellor chore commodore competitor conspirator contributor core corps corridor deplore dinosaur drawer Ecuador editor emperor encore evermore explore exterior floor folklore for fore four furthermore galore governor ignore implore inferior lore matador metaphor more nevermore nor oar offshore or orator ore poor pour rapport restore roar score seashore senator señor shore Singapore snore soar sophomore sore spore store swore therefore Thor tore troubadour underscore uproar visitor whore yore your

Dope (see **Hope**)

Dose adios bellicose close comatose diagnose engross grandiose gross morose nose overdose varicose verbose

Double bubble rubble stubble trouble

Doubt about boy scout blow-out bout clout devout eke out flout gout lout out pout roundabout route scout shout snout spout sprout stout tout trout wash-out worn-out

Dove above glove ladylove love mourning dove of

D

shove turtle dove

Dove by Jove clove cove drove grove rove

Down brown clown crown downtown drown frown gown hand-me-down noun renown town tumble-down upside down uptown

Dozen buzzin' cousin cussin' fusin' musin'

Draft craft draught graft overdraft witchcraft

Drafted grafted shafted (see *did*)

Drag bag brag flag gag hag lag mag nag rag sag shag slag snag stag swag tag wag

Drama Bahama comma Dalai Lama llama mamma melodrama pajama Yokohama

Drank bank blank clank crank dank flank frank hank outrank plank prank rank sank shrank spank stank tank thank yank

Drastic bombastic elastic enthusiastic fantastic gymnastic iconoclastic plastic sarcastic scholastic spastic

Draw Arkansas awe bra caw claw flaw gnaw guffaw hurrah jaw law Ma macaw nah overdraw Pa paw raw saw seesaw shah slaw squaw straw thaw withdraw

Drawn (see **Dawn**)

Dread (see **Said**)

Dream beam cream deem esteem extreme gleam ream regime scheme scream seam seen steam stream supreme team teem

Dreamt attempt contempt exempt tempt unkempt

Dreamy creamy seamy steamy (see *me*)

Dress (see **Confess**)

Dressy messy

Drew (see **Do**)

Drift gift lift shift spendthrift swift thrift

Drill (see **Fill**)

Drink blink brink chink clink fink hoodwink ink kink
link mink pink rink shrink sink slink stink wink
zinc

Drizzle chisel fizzle frizzle grizzle sizzle swizzle

Drop chop cop crop eavesdrop flop hop lollipop
mop plop pop prop raindrop shop stop swap
tip-top whop

Drove by Jove clove cove dove grove rove

Drug bug dug jug hug lug mug plug pug rug shrug
slug smug snug thug tug

Drum (see **Dumb**)

Drummer comer dumber hummer newcomer
strummer summer

Drunk bunk chunk clunk cyberpunk dunk flunk funk
hunk junk monk plunk punk shrunk skunk slunk
spunk stunk sunk trunk

Drunken shrunken sunken

Prefixes: pre, re, in, con, de, mis

D

Dry   alibi amplify banzai barfly butterfly buy by bye certify clarify crucify cry defy deify deny die dignify diversify dragonfly drive-by dye eye firefly fly fry glorify gratify guy high horrify I identify imply July justify lie lullaby modify my mystify notify passerby pie pry qualify rely rye satisfy sci-fi shy sigh signify simplify sky sly specify spry spy terrify testify thigh tie try underlie verify why

Duce   (see **Abuse**)

Duck   (see **Truck**)

Dude   (see **Feud**, **Mood**)

Dudgeon   bludgeon

Due   (see **Knew**)

Duel   cruel fuel jewel perusal renewal

Dug   bug drug jug hug lug mug plug pug rug shrug slug smug snug thug tug

Duke   juke puke uke

Dull   annul cull gull hull lull mull scull skull

Dumb   album aquarium auditorium become bum burdensome Christendom come cranium crematorium crumb curriculum drum emporium fee-fi-fo-fum glum gum gymnasium hum kettledrum kingdom martyrdom maximum meddlesome medium millennium minimum mum museum numb opium overcome pendulum petroleum platinum plum premium quarrelsome radium random rum sanitarium scum slum some strum succumb sum swum tedium thumb Tom Thumb Tweedledum uranium worrisome yum

Dummy crummy gummy mummy rummy tummy yummy

Dump bump chump clump hump jump lump plump rump slump stump thump trump ump

Dupe coop droop group hoop loop nincompoop poop scoop sloop soup stoop swoop troop troupe whoop

Duplex complex decks ex flex necks pecks reflex Rolidex sex specs Tex unisex

During alluring assuring blurring concurring conferring curing deferring demurring deterring enduring ensuring incurring inferring insuring interring luring maturing occurring preferring procuring purring referring securing spurring transferring whirring

Dusk husk musk tusk

Duty beauty cutie

Dwarf wharf

Dwindle kindle rekindle spindle swindle

Dynamic ceramic Islamic panoramic

E

E

Each beach breach impeach leech peach preach reach screech speech teach

Eager beleaguer intriguer leaguer meager overeager

Eagle beagle illegal legal regal sea gull

Ear adhere appear atmosphere auctioneer beer bombardier career cashier cavalier chandelier cheer clear dear deer disappear engineer fear financier frontier gear hear hemisphere here insincere interfere jeer lavaliere leer mere mountaineer near overhear overseer peer persevere pioneer queer racketeer reappear rear revere seer severe shear sheer sincere smear sneer spear sphere stratosphere tear veneer volunteer year

Earn adjourn burn churn concern discern fern intern kern learn overturn return sojourn spurn stern taciturn turn urn yearn

Earth birth dearth girth mirth worth

Ease aborigines appease bees breeze cheese disease expertise freeze Hercules keys knees peas pleas please sees seize Siamese sleaze squeeze tease trapeze 'zzzs

Easel diesel measle weasel

East beast ceased creased deceased feast least

pieced priest yeast

Easy breezy cheesy greasy queasy sleazy sneezy speakeasy wheezy

Eat athlete beat beet bittersweet bleat cheat compete complete conceit concrete deceit defeat delete deplete discreet discrete elite feat feet fleet greet heat incomplete indiscreet meat meet mistreat neat obsolete parakeet receipt repeat retreat seat sheet sleet street suite sweet treat wheat

Ebb deb web

Ebony (see **Be**)

Echo art deco deco gecko (see *glow*)

Ecstasy (see **Be**)

Eden leadin' needin' readin' seedin' Sweden weedin'

Edge allege dredge fledge hedge ledge privilege sacrilege sledge wedge

Educate (see **Ate**)

Effect affect architect bisect checked collect connect correct defect deflect dialect direct disinfect dissect eject erect expect genuflect incorrect inject neglect object pecked perfect project prospect protect recollect reflect reject respect select subject suspect wrecked

Either breather neither

Elapse caps collapse craps flaps lapse maps naps
   perhaps saps traps wraps

Election (see **Affection**)

E

Elf herself himself itself myself self shelf yourself

Elm helm realm overwhelm whelm

Elope (see **Hope**)

Embargo argot cargo Fargo largo

Embrace ace base bass brace case chase
   commonplace debase disgrace displace encase
   erase face grace lace mace misplace pace place
   race replace space steeplechase trace unlace
   vase

Emerge (see **Verge**)

Emotion commotion locomotion lotion motion
   notion ocean potion promotion

Emperor (see **Door**)

Enchant (see **Ant**)

Encore (see **Door**)

End apprehend ascend attend befriend bend blend
   commend comprehend condescend defend
   depend descend dividend expend extend fend
   friend intend lend mend offend penned
   pretend recommend send spend suspend tend
   transcend trend unbend

Ended amended apprehended ascended attended

befriended bended blended commended
comprehended condescended contended
defended depended descended expended
extended fended intended mended
misapprehended offended portended
pretended recommended splendid suspended
tended unattended unblended

Endurance assurance insurance

Endure (see **Cure**)

Enemy (see **Be**)

Energy (see **Be**)

Enjoy ahoy annoy boy buoy convoy corduroy coy
decoy destroy employ Illinois joy ploy Roy
Savoy soy toy troy viceroy

Enough bluff buff cuff duff fluff gruff huff muff
powder puff rough scruff scuff snuff stuff tough

Enter center dissenter experimenter frequenter
inventor mentor presenter preventer renter
tormenter

Entry gentry sentry

Envelope (see **Hope**)

Episode (see **Road**)

Equal sequel

Equation abrasion dissuasion evasion invasion
occasion persuasion

Erase (see **Embrace**)

Erect (see **Effect**)

Erotic chaotic exotic hypnotic idiotic macrobiotic
     narcotic neurotic quixotic

Erratic (see **Attic**)

Error bearer carer darer terror wearer

Erupt abrupt corrupt cupped disrupt interrupt
     supped

Escape ape cape cityscape drape grape landscape
     rape seascape shape tape

Essence adolescence convalescence fluorescence
     incandescence obsolescence

Esteem beam cream deem dream extreme gleam
     ream regime scheme scream seam seen steam
     stream supreme team teem

Eternal colonel external fraternal infernal internal
     journal kernel maternal nocturnal paternal

Eternity fraternity maternity paternity

European Caribbean Crimean Galilean peon (see *in*)

Evangelist (see **Exist**)

Evasive dissuasive invasive persuasive pervasive

Eve achieve believe bereave conceive disbelieve
     grieve heave leave perceive receive relieve
     reprieve retrieve sleeve weave

Evening (see **Sing**)

E

Event (see **Bent**)

Eventful resentful

Everyone anyone begun bun comparison done fun
    Galveston gun hon Hun jettison none nun
    oblivion one outdone outrun overdone overrun
    phenomenon pun run shun simpleton skeleton
    son stun sun ton unison venison won

E

Everything (see **Sing**)

Evict addict conflict constrict contradict convict
    derelict flicked inflict licked predict pricked
    strict

Evil medieval primeval upheaval weevil

Evolution (see **Revolution**)

Ex complex decks duplex flex necks pecks reflex
    Rolidex sex specs Tex unisex

Exact (see **Act**)

Examine famine

Example ample sample trample

Except accept adept crept intercept kept overslept
    slept stepped swept wept

Exception conception contraception deception
    inception perception preconception reception
    self-deception

Excite appetite bite blight bright byte contrite
    copyright daylight delight despite dynamite

Fahrenheit fight flight fright headlight height ignite invite kite knight light midnight might moonlight night outright parasite plight polite quite recite reunite right satellite sight site sleight slight spite starlight sunlight tight trite twilight unite white write

Excuse abuse accuse confuse cues deduce diffuse disuse duce induce infuse introduce juice misuse obtuse peruse produce profuse reduce refuse reproduce seduce Syracuse use

Execution (see **Revolution**)

Exhibit inhibit prohibit

Exist accompanist analyst anarchist anthropologist archeologist assist biologist Calvinist capitalist coexist communist consist cyst desist dismissed egoist essayist evangelist exorcist fatalist gist hissed humanist humorist idealist imperialist insist journalist kissed list lobbyist Methodist missed mist moralist motorist nationalist novelist organist perfectionist pharmacist pianist plagiarist psychologist romanticist satirist sentimentalist socialist soloist specialist strategist terrorist theologist theorist twist ventriloquist vocalist wrist

Existed (see **Twisted**)

Exotic chaotic erotic hypnotic idiotic macrobiotic narcotic neurotic quixotic

Expect (see **Effect**)

Expense (see **Fence**)

Expensive apprehensive comprehensive defensive extensive incomprehensive inexpensive intensive offensive pensive

E

Expert (see **Hurt**)

Explain abstain again airplane arraign ascertain attain brain Cain campaign cane chain champagne cocaine complain contain crane detain disdain domain drain entertain feign gain grain humane hurricane hydroplane insane lane main Maine maintain mane migraine obtain ordain pain pane pertain plain plane profane propane rain refrain reign rein remain sane slain Spain sprain stain strain sustain train vain vane vein wane windowpane

Explode (see **Road**)

Explore (see **Door**)

Export (see **Court**)

Exposure closure composure disclosure foreclosure

Exterior inferior interior superior ulterior

Extinction distinction

Extortion abortion contortion extortion portion proportion

Extreme beam cream deem dream esteem gleam ream regime scheme scream seam seen steam stream supreme team teem

Prefixes: pre, re, in, con, de, mis

Eye alibi amplify banzai barfly butterfly buy by bye certify clarify crucify cry defy deify deny die dignify diversify dragonfly drive-by dry dye firefly fly fry glorify gratify guy high horrify I identify imply July justify lie lullaby modify my mystify notify passerby pie pry qualify rely rye satisfy sci-fi shy sigh signify simplify sky sly specify spry spy terrify testify thigh tie try underlie verify why

Eyes (see **Lies**)

F

Fable (see **Able**)

Face ace base bass brace case chase commonplace debase disgrace displace embrace encase erase grace lace mace misplace pace place race replace space steeplechase trace unlace vase

Facial glacial racial spatial

Fact (see **Act**)

Factor actor benefactor contractor detractor distracter extractor reactor refractor tractor

Factory refractory satisfactory (see *story, be*)

Factual actual contractual

Fade (see **Afraid**)

Fail ale bail bale blackmail braille cocktail curtail exhale female flail frail hail hale impale inhale jail mail male nail pale prevail rail regale sail sale scale shale snail stale tail they'll veil whale

Faint acquaint ain't complaint paint quaint restraint saint taint 'tain't

Fair (see **Air**)

Fairy (see **Cherry**)

Fake ache bake brake break cake flake forsake headache heartache keepsake make mistake opaque quake rake sake shake snake stake steak take wake

F

Fall all ball bawl brawl call crawl doll drawl gall haul install mall maul Montreal nightfall overhaul parasol pitfall protocol rainfall scrawl shawl small snowfall sprawl stall tall thrall wall waterfall y'all

Fame acclaim aim became blame came claim exclaim flame frame game inflame lame maim name proclaim same shame tame

Family (see **Be)**

Famine examine

Famous (see **Us)**

Fantastic bombastic drastic elastic enthusiastic gymnastic iconoclastic plastic sarcastic scholastic spastic

Fantasy (see **Be)**

Far are bar bazaar bizarre car caviar cigar czar disbar guitar jar par scar spar star tar

Farce parse sparse

Farm arm alarm charm disarm forearm harm

Fashion ashen bashin' compassion impassion passion

Fast aghast blast cast classed contrast flabbergast forecast gassed last mast outlast overcast passed past vast

Fat (see **At)**

Fatigue intrigue league

Fatty batty catty chatty Cincinnati natty Patty ratty

Fault assault cobalt exalt halt malt salt somersault vault

Favor braver cadaver favor flavor graver paver saver savor shaver waiver waver

F

Fear adhere appear atmosphere auctioneer beer bombardier career cashier cavalier chandelier cheer clear dear deer disappear ear engineer financier frontier gear hear hemisphere here insincere interfere jeer lavaliere leer mere mountaineer near overhear overseer peer persevere pioneer queer racketeer reappear rear revere seer severe shear sheer sincere smear sneer spear sphere stratosphere tear veneer volunteer year

Feast beast ceased creased deceased east least pieced priest yeast

Feat (see **Sweet**)

Feather altogether Heather leather tether together weather whether (see *her*)

Feature bleacher creature preacher screecher teacher

Fed ahead bed bedspread bread bred coed dead dread figurehead fled flowerbed fountainhead gingerbread head inbred lead led misled misread overfed read red riverbed said shed shred sled sped spread thoroughbred thread underfed unthread wed

Fee (see **Be**)

Feed agreed bleed breed centipede concede creed
deed exceed greed heed inbreed knead lead
mislead need precede proceed read recede
reed secede seed speed stampede succeed
Swede tweed weed

Feel appeal automobile Bastille Camille conceal
deal eel genteel he'll heal heel ideal kneel meal
mobile peel real reel repeal reveal seal she'll
spiel squeal steal steel veal we'll wheal zeal

Feeling appealing ceiling concealing congealing
dealing healing kneeling pealing peeling
reeling repealing revealing squealing stealing
unfeeling wheeling

Feet (see **Sweet**)

Feline beeline sea-line (see *mine*)

Fell bell belle Carmel carrousel cell clientele dell
dwell excel farewell gel hell hotel infidel knell
mademoiselle personnel sell shell smell spell
tell well yell

Fellow bellow cello hello mellow Othello yellow

Felt belt Celt dealt heartfelt melt pelt welt

Female (see **Fail**)

Feminine (see **Been**)

Fence abstinence affluence benevolence

circumference coincidence commence
competence condense conference confidence
consequence convenience defense difference
dispense dissidence eloquence evidence
excellence expense experience frankincense
immense impotence incense incidence
incompetence indigence influence innocence
intense magnificence negligence obedience
permanence preference pretense reference
reverence sense suspense tense violence

Fern (see **Learn**)

Fertile girdle hurdle myrtle turtle

Fetch catch etch kvetch retch sketch stretch wretch

Feud allude altitude aptitude attitude delude dude
fortitude gratitude interlude latitude lewd
longitude magnitude multitude nude prelude
pursued renewed solitude subdued sued 'tude
you'd

Fever achiever beaver believer cleaver deceiver leave
'er receiver reliever retriever weaver

Few (see **Knew**)

Fib ad lib crib glib rib

Fiction addiction affliction benediction
contradiction conviction crucifixion depiction
diction eviction friction jurisdiction prediction
restriction

Fiddle diddle griddle middle riddle twiddle

Field battlefield Chesterfield shield wield yield

Fiend cleaned gleaned meaned quarantined weaned

Fierce pierce

Fiery (see **Be**)

Fight (see **Flight**)

Figment pigment

File aisle awhile beguile bile compile crocodile
defile isle juvenile meanwhile mile Nile pile
rile smile style tile vile while wile worthwhile

Fill bill chill daffodil distill drill frill fulfill gill grill hill
ill imbecile instill kill mill nil quill shrill sill
skill spill still swill thrill till trill until
whippoorwill will windmill windowsill

Final spinal vinyl

Finance advance ants chance circumstance dance
enhance extravagance France glance lance
pants prance romance stance trance

Fine align asinine assign benign combine concubine
confine consign decline define design dine
divine entwine incline line malign mine nine
outshine pine porcupine recline refine resign
Rhine shine shrine sign spine stein swine twine
underline undermine vine whine wine

Finger linger

Finish diminish Finnish

Fire acquire admire amplifier aspire attire buyer

choir conspire crier cryer desire dire drier dryer
entire esquire expire flier friar higher hire
inquire inspire justifier liar magnifier multiplier
mystifier perspire prior prophesier require
retire satisfier sire squire supplier testifier tire
transpire wire

Firm affirm confirm germ reaffirm sperm squirm
term worm

First burst cursed nursed outburst thirst versed
worst

Fish devilish dish gibberish impoverish squish swish
wish

Fishy squishy swishy

Fit befit bit 'git grit kit knit hit it lit nit-wit pit quit sit
spit twit unfit wit zit

Fix acrobatics bics crucifix fiddlesticks kicks licks
mathematics mix nix picks politics six sticks
Styx ticks transfix tricks wicks

Fixture mixture

Fizz biz friz his is quiz showbiz 'tis whiz

Fizzle chisel drizzle frizzle grizzle sizzle swizzle

Flag bag brag drag gag hag lag mag nag rag sag shag
slag snag stag swag tag wag

Flannel channel panel

Flap cap chap clap flap gap handicap lap map
mishap nap rap sap scrap slap snap strap tap

trap wrap zap

Flash ash balderdash bash brash cash clash crash dash gnash rash rehash slash smash splash stash thrash trash

Flat (see **At**)

Flattery battery (see *be*)

Flaunt daunt gaunt haunt jaunt taunt want

Flea (see **Be**)

Flesh enmesh fresh mesh refresh

Flew (see **Do**)

Flick (see **Kick**)

Flight appetite bite blight bright byte contrite copyright daylight delight despite dynamite excite Fahrenheit fight fright headlight height ignite invite kite knight light midnight might moonlight night outright parasite plight polite quite recite reunite right satellite sight site sleight slight spite starlight sunlight tight trite twilight unite white write

Flip battleship chip clip dip drip equip grip gyp hip lip nip quip rip scrip ship slip snip strip tip trip whip zip

Flirt alert avert blurt concert convert curt desert dessert dirt divert exert expert extrovert insert introvert invert pervert shirt skirt squirt subvert yogurt

Float (see **Boat**)

Flock (see **Clock**)

Flood blood bud cud dud mud scud spud stud thud

Floor abhor ambassador ashore auditor bachelor
Baltimore before boar bore chancellor chore
commodore competitor conspirator
contributor core corps corridor deplore
dinosaur door drawer Ecuador editor emperor
encore evermore explore exterior folklore for
fore four furthermore galore governor ignore
implore inferior lore matador metaphor more
nevermore nor oar offshore or orator ore poor
pour rapport restore roar score seashore
senator señor shore Singapore snore soar
sophomore sore spore store swore therefore
Thor tore troubadour underscore uproar visitor
whore yore your

Flop (see **Drop**)

Flour devour hour our scour (see *flower*)

Flourish amateurish nourish

Flow afro although banjo beau below bestow blow
bow buffalo bungalow calico crossbow crow
depot doe domino dough embryo escrow
Eskimo foe forgo fro gazebo gigolo glow go
grow heigh-ho ho-ho hobo hoe incognito
indigo Joe know long ago low Mexico mistletoe
mow no oboe oh outgrow overflow overgrow
overthrow owe Pinocchio pistachio plateau quo

F

rainbow ratio roe row sew slow snow so Soho status quo stow studio tally-ho though throw tiptoe to-and-fro toe Tokyo tow tremolo undergo undertow vertigo woe yo yo-yo

F

Flower cauliflower cower deflower empower horsepower plower power shower tower (see *our*)

Flowery bowery dowry floury flowery showery

Flowing blowing bowing crowing glowing going growing hoeing knowing mowing overflowing owing rowing sewing showing slowing snowing sowing stowing throwing towing

Flown (see **Known**)

Fluffy huffy puffy stuffy

Fluke kook spook

Flunk bunk chunk clunk cyberpunk drunk dunk funk hunk junk monk plunk punk shrunk skunk slunk spunk stunk sunk trunk

Flute (see **Cute**)

Fly alibi amplify banzai barfly butterfly buy by bye certify clarify crucify cry defy deify deny die dignify diversify dragonfly drive-by dry dye eye firefly fry glorify gratify guy high horrify I identify imply July justify lie lullaby modify my mystify notify passerby pie pry qualify rely rye satisfy sci-fi shy sigh signify simplify sky sly specify spry spy terrify testify thigh tie try underlie verify why

Focus hocus-pocus locus (see *us*)

Foe (see **Blow**)

Fog analog bog catalog clog cog demagogue
dialogue dog epilogue flog frog grog hog hot
dog jog log monologue prairie dog synagogue
travelogue

Foggy doggy froggy groggy soggy

Foil broil coil loyal oil recoil royal spoil toil turmoil

Fold behold blindfold bold centerfold cold foothold
foretold gold hold household marigold mold
old retold scold sold told uphold withhold

Folk (see **Joke**)

Follow Apollo hollow swallow wallow

Folly collie dolly finale golly jolly melancholy Molly
Polly tamale trolley volley

Fond beyond blond bond correspond dawned pond
respond spawned vagabond wand yawned

Food brood clued conclude crude dude exclude
glued include intrude misconstrued mood
preclude prude rude seclude shrewd wooed

Fool April fool cool drool ghoul Liverpool overrule
pool rule school spool stool tool whirlpool

Foot afoot leadfoot pussyfoot tenderfoot put

For (see **Door**)

F

Forbid bid did grid hid invalid lid Madrid pyramid rid skid slid squid

Ford (see **Lord**)

Foreclosure closure composure disclosure exposure

Forever clever endeavor ever however lever never sever whatever whenever wherever whoever

Forge George gorge

Forget alphabet bayonet bet brunette cabinet cadet cigarette clarinet cornet corvette debt duet epithet etiquette fret gazette get jet Joliet Juliet let luncheonette marionette met net omelet pet quartet regret roulette set silhouette Somerset sunset sweat threat Tibet toilette upset vet 'vette violet wet yet

Forgiven driven given (see *in*)

Forgotten begotten cotten gotten rotten

Fork cork New York pork torque stork uncork

Form chloroform conform deform inform norm perform rainstorm reform snowstorm storm swarm transform uniform warm

Formal abnormal informal normal

Fort (see **Court**)

Forth fourth henceforth north

Fossil apostle colossal docile jostle

Fought astronaut bought brought caught cosmonaut fought naught ought overwrought sought taught thought wrought

Foul   cowl foul growl howl jowl owl prowl scowl
waterfowl

Found   abound around astound background
battleground bloodhound bound compound
confound downed dumbfound ground hound
impound merry-go-round mound pound
profound renowned resound round sound
spellbound surround underground wound

Foundry   boundary

Fox   box chickenpox equinox mailbox orthodox ox
paradox

Fragile   agile (see *smile, fill*)

Fragrance   flagrance vagrants

Frantic   antic Atlantic chromatic gigantic pedantic
romantic transatlantic

Fraternity   eternity maternity paternity

Fraud   abroad applaud awed broad clod cod defraud
façade God guffawed Izod nod odd pod prod
promenade quad rod roughshod shod sod
squad trod wad

Freak   beak bleak creek eek leak meek reek seek
speak tweak weak week

Freckle   heckle speckle

Freeze   (see **Ease**)

Frequence   sequence

F

Fresh enmesh flesh mesh refresh

Friction affliction benediction contradiction
conviction crucifixion depiction diction
eviction fiction jurisdiction prediction
restriction

Friend apprehend ascend attend befriend bend
blend commend comprehend condescend
defend depend descend dividend end expend
extend fend intend lend mend offend penned
pretend recommend send spend suspend tend
transcend trend unbend

Fright (see **Flight**)

Frigid rigid

Fringe binge cringe hinge infringe singe

Frisky risky whiskey

Frog analog bog catalog clog cog fog demagogue
dialogue dog epilogue frog grog hog jog log
monologue synagogue travelogue

Front affront blunt brunt bunt confront forefront
grunt hunt punt runt shunt stunt

Frost bossed cost crossed exhaust flossed holocaust
lost Pentecost tossed

Frown brown clown crown down downtown drown
frown gown hand-me-down noun renown town
tumble-down upside down uptown

Froze arose chose close compose decompose
depose disclose dispose doze enclose expose

foreclose goes hose impose indispose
interpose knows nose owes pose predispose
presuppose prose recompose rose suppose
those toes transpose woes

Frozen chosen dozin' mosin' nosin' posin'

F

Fruit (see **Cute**)

Frustrate (see **Ate**)

Fry (see **Cry**)

Fuel cruel duel jewel

Fuel duel perusal renewal

Fun anyone begun bun comparison done everyone
Galveston gun hon Hun jettison none nun
oblivion one outdone outrun overdone overrun
phenomenon pun run shun simpleton skeleton
son stun sun ton unison venison won

Function conjunction junction injunction

Fund cummerbund refund rotund shunned

Funky chunky flunky monkey spunky

Funny bunny honey sunny

Fur (see **Her**)

Fury curry flurry hurry jury Missouri scurry slurry
surrey worry

Fuss (see **Us**)

Future suture

Fuzz abuzz buzz cause coz does was

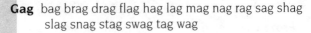

G

Gag bag brag drag flag hag lag mag nag rag sag shag slag snag stag swag tag wag

Gain abstain again airplane arraign ascertain attain brain Cain campaign cane chain champagne cocaine complain contain crane detain disdain domain drain entertain explain feign grain humane hurricane hydroplane insane lane main Maine maintain mane migraine obtain ordain pain pane pertain plain plane profane propane rain refrain reign rein remain sane slain Spain sprain stain strain sustain train vain vane vein wane windowpane

Gal canal chorale morale pal shall

Galaxy (see **Be**)

Gallery calorie Mallory salary

Gamble amble ramble scramble shamble

Garage barrage camouflage entourage mirage

Garden harden pardon

Gasoline (see **Mean**)

Gasp asp clasp grasp

Gave behave brave cave concave crave engrave forgave grave knave pave rave save shave slave waive wave

Gavel gravel ravel travel unravel

Gawk (see **Clock**)

Gaze ablaze amaze appraise bays blaze braze craze
    days daze faze glaze graze haze malaise
    mayonnaise maze nays nowadays plays
    polonaise praise ways

Geese cease crease decease decrease fleece grease
    Greece increase lease mantelpiece masterpiece
    peace piece police release

Gem Bethlehem condemn hem phlegm requiem
    stem them

Gender (see **Tender**)

Generic atmospheric cleric Derrick esoteric
    hemispheric hysteric numeric

Gentle accidental coincidental complemental
    compliment continental dental departmental
    detrimental experimental fundamental
    governmental incidental intercontinental lentil
    mental monumental Oriental parental
    regimental rental rudimental sentimental
    supplemental temperamental

Gently evidently impotently innocently insolently
    intently

Germ affirm confirm firm reaffirm sperm squirm
    term worm

Get alphabet bayonet bet brunette cabinet cadet

cigarette clarinet cornet corvette debt duet
epithet etiquette forget fret gazette jet Joliet
Juliet let luncheonette marionette met net
omelet pet quartet regret roulette set
silhouette Somerset sunset sweat threat Tibet
toilette upset vet 'vette violet wet yet

Ghetto allegretto amoretto falsetto libretto stiletto

Ghost boast coast foremost furthermost host
innermost most post roast toast whipping post

Giant client compliant defiant reliant self-reliant

Gift drift lift shift spendthrift swift thrift

Giggle jiggle squiggle wiggle wriggle

Gigolo bolo piccolo polo solo tremolo

Gin aspirin been begin Berlin bin chagrin chin
discipline feminine fin genuine grin harlequin
heroine in inn kin mandolin mannequin
masculine moccasin origin pin saccharine shin
sin skin spin thick-and-thin thin tin twin violin
win within

Ginger injure infringer

Girl curl earl hurl pearl swirl twirl whirl

Give affirmative alternative argumentative
combative competitive consecutive
conservative definitive expletive figurative
forgive fugitive informative intuitive live
lucrative narrative negative positive primitive

prohibitive provocative relative representative sensitive talkative tentative

Glad ad add bad Brad cad Chad clad Dad egad fad grad had lad mad nomad pad plaid sad shad Trinidad

Glamorous amorous clamorous (see *us*)

Glamour clamor damn 'er grammar hammer slammer sledgehammer stammer yammer

Glance advance ants chance circumstance dance enhance extravagance finance France lance pants prance romance stance trance

Glass (see **Class**)

Glitter bitter counterfeiter critter fitter fritter litter quitter sitter transmitter twitter (see *her*)

Gloat (see **Boat**)

Globe disrobe Job probe robe strobe

Gloom bloom boom broom cloakroom doom entomb flume groom room tomb whom womb zoom

Glorify horrify

Glory accusatory allegory category dormitory dory gory hunky-dory laboratory Lori obligatory observatory oratory Peter Lorre quarry reformatory retaliatory sorry story territory Tory

Glove above dove ladylove love mourning dove of shove turtle dove

Glow   afro although banjo beau below bestow blow
bow buffalo bungalow calico crossbow crow
depot doe domino dough embryo escrow
Eskimo flow foe forgo fro gazebo gigolo go
grow heigh ho ho-ho hobo hoe incognito
indigo Joe know long-ago low Mexico mistletoe
mow no oboe oh outgrow overflow overgrow
overthrow owe Pinocchio pistachio plateau quo
rainbow ratio roe row sew slow snow so Soho
status quo stow studio tally-ho though throw
tiptoe to-and-fro toe Tokyo tow tremolo
undergo undertow vertigo woe yo yo-yo

Glue   (see **Do**)

Glum   album aquarium auditorium become bum
burdensome Christendom come cranium
crematorium crumb curriculum drum dumb
emporium fee-fi-fo-fum gum gymnasium hum
kettledrum kingdom martyrdom maximum
meddlesome medium millennium minimum
mum museum numb opium overcome
pendulum petroleum platinum plum premium
quarrelsome radium random rum sanitarium
scum slum some strum succumb sum swum
tedium thumb Tom Thumb Tweedledum
uranium worrisome yum

Glut   (see **But**)

Gnarl   Carl snarl

Go   afro although banjo beau below bestow blow

bow buffalo bungalow calico crossbow crow
depot doe domino dough embryo escrow
Eskimo flow foe forgo fro gazebo gigolo glow
grow heigh ho ho-ho hobo hoe incognito
indigo Joe know long-ago low Mexico mistletoe
mow no oboe oh outgrow overflow overgrow
overthrow owe Pinocchio pistachio plateau quo
rainbow ratio roe row sew slow snow so Soho
status quo stow studio tally-ho though throw
tiptoe to-and-fro toe Tokyo tow tremolo
undergo undertow vertigo woe yo yo-yo

Goal (see **Hole**)

God abroad applaud awed broad clod cod defraud
façade fraud guffawed Izod nod odd pod prod
promenade quad rod roughshod shod sod
squad trod wad

Goggle boggle boondoggle toggle

Gold behold blindfold bold centerfold cold fold
foothold foretold hold household marigold
mold old retold scold sold told uphold
withhold

Golly collie dolly finale folly jolly melancholy Molly
Polly tamale trolley volley

Gone Amazon autobahn Babylon bonbon Bonn
brawn chiffon con dawn drawn echelon fawn
lawn neon on pawn pentagon silicon swan
undergone upon wan woebegone wonton yawn

Good brotherhood could fatherhood firewood Hollywood hood likelihood livelihood misunderstood motherhood neighborhood should sisterhood stood understood withstood womanhood wood would

Goose caboose loose moose noose papoose recluse spruce truce vamoose

Gorilla guerrilla Manila Priscilla vanilla villa

Gory (see **Story**)

Gown (see **Clown**)

Grab blab cab crab dab drab gab jab lab nab scab slab stab tab

Grace ace base bass brace case chase commonplace debase disgrace displace embrace encase erase face lace mace misplace pace place race replace space steeplechase trace unlace vase

Grade aid arcade afraid barricade blade blockade braid brayed brigade centigrade charade crusade degrade dismayed dissuade downgrade escapade evade fade grenade hayed invade laid lemonade made maid masquerade paid parade persuade played promenade raid renegade serenade shade spade stockade suede tirade trade

Grain (see **Insane**)

Gram (see **Am**)

G

Granny Annie canny fanny nanny

Grape ape cape cityscape drape escape landscape
rape seascape shape tape

Graph calf carafe epitaph giraffe paragraph
phonograph photograph polygraph riffraff staff
telegraph

G

Grasp asp clasp gasp

Grass alas amass ass bass brass class crass gas
glass harass hourglass lass looking-glass mass
morass mustache overpass pass sass sassafras
surpass

Gratitude attitude latitude platitude

Grave behave brave cave concave crave engrave
forgave gave knave pave rave save shave slave
waive wave

Gravel gavel ravel travel unravel

Gravity cavity depravity

Greed agreed breed centipede concede creed deed
exceed feed heed inbreed knead lead mislead
need precede proceed read recede reed secede
seed speed stampede succeed Swede tweed
weed

Greedy beady needy seedy speedy weedy (see *be*)

Green (see **Mean**)

Greet athlete beat beet bittersweet bleat cheat
compete complete conceit concrete deceit

defeat delete deplete discreet discrete eat elite
feat feet fleet heat incomplete indiscreet meat
meet mistreat neat obsolete parakeet receipt
repeat retreat seat sheet sleet street suite
sweet treat wheat

Grew (see **Do**)

Grief beef belief brief chief disbelief leaf relief thief

Grieve achieve believe bereave conceive disbelieve
eve heave leave perceive receive relieve
reprieve retrieve sleeve weave

Grill bill chill daffodil distill drill fill frill fulfill gill hill
ill imbecile instill kill mill nil quill shrill sill
skill spill still swill thrill till trill until
whippoorwill will windmill windowsill

Grim brim dim gym him hymn limb pseudonym skim
slim swim trim whim

Grin aspirin been begin Berlin bin chagrin chin
discipline feminine fin genuine gin harlequin
heroine in inn kin mandolin mannequin
masculine moccasin origin pin saccharine shin
sin skin spin thick-and-thin thin tin twin violin
win within

Grip (see **Trip**)

Grocer closer (see *sir*)

Groin coin Des Moines join loin purloin sirloin
tenderloin

Gross adios bellicose close comatose diagnose dose engross grandiose morose nose overdose varicose verbose

Grouch couch crouch ouch pouch slouch vouch

Ground (see **Found**)

Group coop droop dupe hoop loop nincompoop poop scoop sloop soup stoop swoop troop troupe whoop

Grovel hovel novel

Grow (see **Glow**)

Grown (see **Known**)

Growth both loath oath overgrowth undergrowth

Guard avant-garde card chard discard disregard hard lard regard retard tarred yard

Guess access address baroness bashfulness bitterness bless caress chess cleverness cloudiness compress confess craziness deadliness depress digress distress dizziness dress duress eagerness easiness eeriness emptiness excess express finesse foolishness ghostliness happiness haziness homelessness idleness impress joyfulness joylessness laziness less limitless Loch Ness lustfulness mess nervousness obsess openness oppress outrageousness penniless playfulness possess press profess progress queasiness recess regress repossess repress rockiness seediness shallowness silkiness sleaziness sleepiness sneakiness SOS spaciousness spitefulness stress success suppress thoughtfulness transgress uselessness viciousness willingness wishfulness worldliness yes youthfulness

Guest (see **Best**)

Guilt built hilt jilt kilt quilt spilt stilt tilt Vanderbilt wilt

Guitar are bar bazaar bizarre car caviar cigar czar disbar far jar par scar spar star tar

Gulch mulch

Gull annul cull dull hull lull mull scull skull

Gum (see **Dumb**)

Gun anyone begun bun comparison done everyone fun Galveston hon Hun jettison none nun oblivion one outdone outrun overdone overrun phenomenon pun run shun simpleton skeleton son stun sun ton unison venison won

Guppy puppy yuppie

Gust (see **Trust**)

Gut but butt cut glut halibut hut King Tut mutt nut putt rut scuttlebutt shut slut smut strut uncut

Gutter butter clutter cutter flutter mutter putter shutter sputter strutter stutter utter

Guy alibi amplify banzai barfly butterfly buy by bye certify clarify crucify defy deify deny die dignify

diversify dragonfly drive-by dry dye eye firefly
fly fry glorify gratify high horrify I identify imply
July justify lie lullaby modify my mystify notify
passerby pie pry qualify rely rye satisfy sci-fi
shy sigh signify simplify sky sly specify spry spy
terrify testify thigh tie try underlie verify why

Gypsy   dipsy Poughkeepsie tipsy

G

guy

certify

gypsy

tipsy

guppy

puppy

H

Had ad add bad Brad cad Chad clad Dad egad fad
glad grad lad mad nomad pad plaid sad shad
Trinidad

Hail (see **Ale**)

Hair (see **Air**)

Hairy carry hari-kari marry miscarry parry vary (see
cherry)

Hallow callow fallow mallow marshmallow shallow
tallow

Halloween (see **Mean**)

Halt assault cobalt exalt fault malt salt somersault
vault

Hammer clamor damn 'er glamour grammar
slammer sledgehammer stammer yammer

Hand and band brand canned command contraband
demand expand fanned grand land panned
planned reprimand Rio Grande sand stand

Handle candle dandle sandal scandal vandal

Handy Andy brandy candy dandy randy sandy

Hanky cranky lanky Yankee

Happiness (see **Guess**)

Happy crappie nappy pappy sappy scrappy
slaphappy yappy

Harbor arbor barber (see *door*)

Hard avant-garde card chard discard disregard guard
  lard regard retard tarred yard

Hark aardvark arc ark bark dark embark lark mark
  narc park patriarch remark shark spark stark

Harm arm alarm charm disarm farm forearm

Harmonic catatonic chronic diatonic enharmonic
  ironic monophonic philharmonic phonic
  platonic polyphonic sonic symphonic tonic

Harmonica Monica Santa Monica Veronica

Harp carp sharp

Harsh marsh

Has as jazz razzmatazz whereas

Haste baste aftertaste braced chaste distaste faced
  freckle-faced hatchet-faced lambaste paste
  taste waist waste

Hat (see **At**)

Hatch attach batch catch detach dispatch latch
  match patch scratch snatch

Hatchet latchet ratchet

Hate (see **Ate**)

Hated anticipated bated belated dated fated grated
  mated rated related sedated skated x-rated
  (see **Ate(d)**)

Haunt daunt flaunt gaunt jaunt taunt want

Haunting daunting flaunting jaunting taunting
    vaunting wanting

Have calve

Hawk (see **Clock**)

Haze ablaze amaze appraise bays blaze braze craze
    days daze faze gaze glaze graze malaise
    mayonnaise maze nays nowadays plays
    polonaise praise ways

Hazel appraisal nasal

Hazy crazy daisy lazy

He (see **Be**)

Head ahead bed bedspread bread bred coed dead
    dread fed figurehead fled flowerbed
    fountainhead gingerbread inbred lead led
    misled misread overfed read red riverbed said
    shed shred sled sped spread thoroughbred
    thread underfed unthread wed

Heal appeal automobile Bastille Camille conceal
    deal eel feel genteel he'll heel ideal kneel meal
    mobile peel real reel repeal reveal seal she'll
    spiel squeal steal steel veal we'll wheal zeal

Healer congealer dealer feeler reeler sealer squealer
    stealer wheeler

Health commonwealth stealth wealth

Hear (see **Near**)

Heard absurd bird blackbird bluebird curd herd

hummingbird ladybird mockingbird overheard third word yellowbird

Hearse   adverse converse curse disburse disperse diverse immerse intersperse inverse nurse purse rehearse reverse terse transverse traverse universe verse worse

Heart   apart art cart chart counterpart dart depart mart part smart start sweetheart tart upstart

Heartache   (see **Ache**)

Heat   (see **Sweet**)

Heaven   eleven leaven seven

Heavy   bevy Chevy levee

Heck   check Czech deck fleck neck peck Quebec speck trek wreck

Height   (see **Flight**)

Heist   Christ diced feist iced zeitgeist

Held   felled meld upheld weld

Hell   bell belle Carmel carrousel cell clientele dell dwell excel farewell fell gel hotel infidel knell mademoiselle personnel sell shell smell spell tell well yell

Hellbound   hellhound spellbound (see *found*)

Hellfire   shellfire (see *fire*)

Hellish   embellish relish

Hello   bellow cello fellow mellow Othello yellow

Prefixes: pre, re, in, con, de, mis

Help　kelp yelp

Her　amateur blur chauffeur concur confer
connoisseur defer demur deter fur incur infer
Jennifer myrrh occur per prefer purr recur sir
slur spur stir transfer voyageur were whir

Hercules　(see **Ease**)

Here　(see **Near**)

Hero　Nero zero (see *know*)

Hesitative　(see **Native**)

Hey　(see **Say**)

Hid　bid did forbid grid invalid lid Madrid pyramid rid
skid slid squid

Hide　beside bonafide bride collide confide
countryside decide defied died dignified divide
eyed fireside guide hillside homicide inside
lied outside override pride provide reside ride
side slide snide stride subdivide subside
suicide tide tried wide yuletide

High　(see **Cry**)

Highlight　skylight twilight (see *light*)

Highway　byway skyway (see *way*)

Hijacker　attacker backer blacker cracker hacker
nutcracker packer ransacker slacker smacker
tracker

Hike　bike like mike spike strike tyke

Hilarious Aquarius gregarious precarious Sagittarius various (see *us*)

Hill (see **Fill**)

Hilly Billy Chile Chili chilly dilly filly frilly hillbilly lily Philly Piccadilly piccalilli shrilly silly willy-nilly

Him brim dim grim gym hymn limb pseudonym skim slim swim trim whim

Hinge binge cringe fringe infringe singe

Hint flint lint mint peppermint print spearmint splint sprint squint tint

Hip (see **Trip**)

Hippie chippy dippy drippy flippy Mississippi nippy slippy snippy tippy yippee zippy

Hire (see **Fire**)

His biz fizz friz is quiz showbiz 'tis whiz

Hiss abyss amiss analysis armistice bliss carcass cowardice dismiss emphasis hypothesis kiss miss nemesis office prejudice Swiss synthesis this

History mystery (see *be*)

Hit befit bit fit 'git grit kit knit it lit nit-wit pit quit sit twit unfit wit zit

Hoagie Bogie stogie

Hoard (see **Lord**)

Hoax chokes coax folks jokes polks smokes spokes

yokes

Hobby   bobby knobby lobby snobby (see *be*)

Hold   behold blindfold bold centerfold cold fold
foothold foretold gold household marigold
mold old retold scold sold told uphold
withhold

Hole   bowl buttonhole cajole casserole coal control
dole droll enroll goal loophole Maypole mole
Old King Cole oriole parole patrol pole poll
porthole role roll scroll tadpole toll troll whole

Holiday   (see **Say**)

Hollow   Apollo follow swallow wallow

Hollywood   (see **Good**)

Holy   drolly lowly roly-poly solely wholly

Home   chrome chromosome comb dome foam
gnome honeycomb metronome Nome poem
roam Rome tome

Honesty   (see **Be**)

Honey   bunny funny money sunny

Honolulu   Lulu Zulu

Honor   dishonor goner

Hood   (see **Good**)

Hook   book brook cook crook look mistook nook
outlook rook shook took undertook

Hoop   coop droop dupe group loop nincompoop

poop scoop sloop soup stoop swoop troop troupe whoop

Hope antelope cantaloupe cope dope elope envelope grope gyroscope horoscope kaleidoscope microscope mope pope rope scope slope soap stethoscope telescope

Horn adorn airborne born Cape Horn Capricorn corn lovelorn Matterhorn morn mourn popcorn scorn stillborn sworn unicorn warn worn

Horny corny thorny

Horrify glorify

Horror adorer explorer gorer ignorer restorer roarer snorer soarer (see *her*)

Horse coarse course divorce endorse force Norse reinforce remorse resource source

Hosanna (see **Nirvana**)

Host boast coast foremost furthermost ghost innermost most post roast toast whipping post

Hot apricot blot Camelot clot cot cybot dot forget-me-not forgot fought gavotte got hot-shot jot knot lot not plot pot robot rot shot slingshot somewhat spot squat swat tot trot watt what yacht

Hotel bell belle Carmel carrousel cell clientele dell dwell excel farewell fell gel hell infidel knell mademoiselle personnel sell shell smell spell

H

tell well yell

Hound abound around astound background
battleground bloodhound bound compound
confound downed dumbfound found ground
impound merry-go-round mound pound
profound renowned resound round sound
spellbound surround underground wound

Hour devour flour our scour (see *flower*)

House blouse douse grouse louse madhouse mouse
outhouse penthouse slaughterhouse souse
spouse

How allow avow bough bow brow chow cow disavow
endow frau kowtow now ow plough plow row
slough somehow sow thou vow wow

Howl cowl foul fowl growl jowl owl prowl scowl
waterfowl

Huff (see **Bluff**)

Hug bug drug dug jug lug mug plug pug rug shrug
slug smug snug thug tug

Huge centrifuge Scrooge stooge

Hulk bulk sulk

Human Harry S. Truman Paul Newman (see *man*)

Humble bumble crumble fumble grumble humble
jumble mumble rumble stumble tumble

Humiliate affiliate conciliate

Humor bloomer boomer consumer rumor tumor

Hung (see **Young**)

Hunger fishmonger rumormonger younger (see *her*)

Hunt affront blunt brunt bunt confront forefront front grunt punt runt shunt stunt

Hurdle curdle girdle

Hurricane (see **Insane**)

Hurry curry flurry fury jury Missouri scurry slurry surrey worry

Hurt alert avert blurt concert convert curt desert dessert dirt divert exert expert extrovert flirt insert introvert invert pervert shirt skirt squirt subvert yogurt

Hustle bustle corpuscle muscle mussel rustle tussle

Hype archetype gripe pipe prototype ripe stereotype stripe swipe type wipe

Hysteric atmospheric cleric Derrick esoteric generic hemispheric hysteric numeric

I

I alibi amplify banzai barfly butterfly buy by bye
    certify clarify crucify cry defy deify deny die
    dignify diversify dragonfly drive-by dry dye eye
    firefly fly fry glorify gratify guy high horrify I
    identify imply July justify lie lullaby modify my
    mystify notify passerby pie pry qualify rely rye
    satisfy sci-fi shy sigh signify simplify sky sly
    specify spry spy terrify testify thigh tie try
    underlie verify why

Ice advice concise device dice entice lice mice nice
    paradise precise price rice sacrifice spice splice
    suffice thrice twice vice

Icicle bicycle tricycle

Icy dicey spicy

Idealist (see **Exist**)

Idiot (see **It**)

Idol bridal bridle homicidal idle suicidal tidal

If cliff handkerchief sniff stiff tiff whiff

Iffy jiffy sniffy spiffy

Ignore (see **Door**)

Ill bill chill daffodil distill drill fill frill fulfill gill grill
    hill imbecile instill kill mill nil quill shrill sill
    skill spill still swill thrill till trill until

whippoorwill will windmill windowsill

Illusion allusion conclusion confusion delusion
fusion inclusion infusion seclusion transfusion

Image scrimmage

Imitative (see **Native**)

Immature (see **Cure**)

Impostor accoster foster lost 'er roster

Impressive aggressive depressive digressive
excessive expressive possessive progressive
regressive successive

In aspirin been begin Berlin bin chagrin chin
discipline feminine fin genuine gin grin
harlequin heroine inn kin mandolin
mannequin masculine moccasin origin pin
saccharine shin sin skin spin thick-and-thin
thin tin twin violin win within

Inch cinch flinch lynch pinch

Include brood clued conclude crude dude exclude
food glued intrude misconstrued mood
preclude prude rude seclude shrewd wooed

Increase cease crease decease decrease fleece
geese grease Greece lease mantelpiece
masterpiece peace piece police release

Independent ascendant attendant defendant
dependent descendant independent pendant
superintendent transcendent

Individual residual

Indulge bulge divulge

Industry (see **Be**)

Infatuate (see **Ate**)

Inferior exterior interior superior ulterior

Infernal colonel eternal external fraternal internal journal kernel maternal nocturnal paternal

Inflict addict conflict constrict contradict convict derelict evict flicked licked predict pricked strict

Influence (see **Fence**)

Influential confidential credential deferential differential essential existential nonessential potential preferential presidential providential prudential quintessential residential sequential torrential

Inherit demerit disinherit (see *it*)

Initial artificial beneficial judicial official sacrificial superficial

Injure ginger infringer

Injury (see **Be**)

Ink blink brink chink clink drink fink kink link mink pink rink shrink sink slink stink wink zinc

Innuendo crescendo diminuendo Nintendo (see *know*)

Insane abstain again airplane arraign ascertain attain brain Cain campaign cane chain champagne cocaine complain contain crane detain disdain domain drain entertain explain feign gain grain humane hurricane hydroplane lane main Maine maintain mane migraine obtain ordain pain pane pertain plain plane profane propane rain refrain reign rein remain sane slain Spain sprain stain strain sustain train vain vane vein wane windowpane

Insecure (see **Cure**)

Insert (see **Hurt**)

Insist accompanist analyst anarchist anthropologist archeologist assist biologist Calvinist capitalist coexist communist consist cyst desist dismissed egoist essayist evangelist exist exorcist fatalist gist hissed humanist humorist idealist imperialist journalist kissed list lobbyist Methodist missed mist moralist motorist nationalist novelist organist perfectionist pharmacist pianist plagiarist psychologist romanticist satirist sentimentalist socialist soloist specialist strategist terrorist theologist theorist twist ventriloquist vocalist wrist

Insisted (see **Twisted**)

Inspector collector connector deflector detector director injector nectar objector projector

prospector protector reflector selector vector
(see *her*)

Inspiration congregational creational educational
recreational sensational

Inspire acquire admire amplifier aspire attire buyer
choir conspire crier cryer desire dire drier dryer
entire esquire expire fire flier friar higher hire
inquire justifier liar magnifier multiplier
mystifier perspire prior prophesier require
retire satisfier sire squire supplier testifier tire
transpire wire

Insurance assurance endurance

Intensive apprehensive comprehensive defensive
expensive extensive incomprehensive
inexpensive offensive pensive

Invasion abrasion dissuasion equation evasion
occasion persuasion

Invent (see **Bent**)

Invention (see **Tension**)

Inventive attentive inattentive incentive retentive

Inventor center dissenter enter experimenter
frequenter mentor presenter preventer renter
tormenter

Invest arrest attest best breast chest congest crest
detest digest divest double-breast infest ingest
interest jest manifest molest nest protest

quest request rest single-breast suggest test vest

Invisible divisible indivisible visible

Invite appetite bite blight bright byte contrite copyright daylight delight despite dynamite excite Fahrenheit fight flight fright headlight height ignite kite knight light midnight might moonlight night outright parasite plight polite quite recite reunite right satellite sight site sleight slight spite starlight sunlight tight trite twilight unite white write

Involve absolve devolve dissolve evolve revolve solve

Irate gyrate (see *rate*)

Ironic catatonic chronic diatonic enharmonic harmonic monophonic philharmonic phonic platonic polyphonic sonic symphonic tonic

Is biz fizz friz his quiz showbiz 'tis whiz

Island highland (see *land*)

Issue tissue (see *you*)

It befit bit fit 'git grit kit knit hit idiot lit nit-wit pit quit sit twit unfit wit zit

Ivory (see **Be**)

I s s tissue

J

Jacket bracket packet racket (see *it*)

Jail ale bail bale blackmail braille cocktail curtail exhale fail female flail frail hail hale impale inhale mail male nail pale prevail rail regale sail sale scale shale snail stale tail they'll veil whale

Jam (see **Am**)

Jar are bar bazaar bizarre car caviar cigar czar disbar far guitar par scar spar star tar

Jaw Arkansas awe bra caw claw draw flaw gnaw guffaw hurrah jaw law Ma macaw nah overdraw Pa paw raw saw seesaw shah slaw squaw straw thaw withdraw

Jazz as has razzmatazz whereas

Jealous tell us zealous (see **Us**)

Jealousy (see **Be**)

Jelly belly deli Kelly Shelly smelly

Jerk clerk handiwork irk Kirk lurk murk overwork perk quirk shirk smirk Turk work

Jester Chester contester fester investor Lester molester pester protester semester sequester tester Westchester Winchester

Jet (see **Met**)

Jewel cruel duel fuel

Jiggle   giggle squiggle wiggle wriggle

Jingle   intermingle Kris Kringle mingle shingle single tingle

Jinx   lynx minks sphinx thinks winks

Job   blob bob cob fob gob hob hobnob job knob lob mob nob rob slob snob sob swab throb

Jock   Bangkok beanstalk boondock clock cock cornstalk crock deadlock defrock dock flintlock flock frock gawk gridlock hawk hock J.S. Bach knock Little Rock livestock lock mock Mohawk padlock peacock rock shock sidewalk small talk smock sock squawk stalk stock talk tomahawk unlock walk wok

Joe   (see **Glow**)

Join   adjoin coin Des Moines groin loin purloin sirloin tenderloin

Joint   anoint appoint counterpoint disappoint disjoint

Joke   artichoke baroque bloke broke choke cloak coke croak evoke folk invoke oak poke provoke revoke smoke soak spoke stroke toke woke yoke

Joker   broker choker mediocre poker provoker revoker smoker stoker stroker woke 'er

Jolly   collie dolly finale folly golly melancholy Molly Polly tamale trolley volley

Jolt   bolt colt dolt revolt thunderbolt

Journal   colonel eternal external fraternal infernal

internal kernel maternal nocturnal paternal

Journalist (see **Exist**)

Journey attorney tourney (see *be*)

Joy ahoy annoy boy buoy convoy corduroy coy decoy
destroy employ enjoy Illinois ploy Roy Savoy
soy toy troy viceroy

Judge budge drudge fudge grudge misjudge nudge
smudge

Juggle smuggle snuggle struggle

Juice (see **Abuse**)

Jumbo gumbo (see *no*)

Jump bump chump clump dump hump lump plump
rump slump stump thump trump ump

Junction conjunction function injunction

June attune commune dune immune impugn
inopportune tune (see *moon*)

Jungle bungle

Junk bunk chunk clunk cyberpunk drunk dunk flunk
funk hunk monk plunk punk shrunk skunk
slunk spunk stunk sunk trunk

Juror deferrer demurrer furor incurrer stirrer (see *her*)

Jury curry flurry fury hurry Missouri scurry slurry
surrey worry

Just adjust August bust crust disgust distrust
encrust entrust gust lust mistrust must robust
rust thrust trust unjust

Juvenile (see **Smile**)

K

Keep barkeep cheep creep deep heap leap peep reap seep sheep sleep steep sweep weep

Keg beg egg leg peg

Kept accept adept crept except intercept overslept slept stepped swept wept

Key (see **Be**)

Kick arithmetic arsenic brick candlestick candlewick Catholic chick click flick heartsick hick lick limerick love-sick lunatic maverick nick pick sick slick stick thick tic tick wick

Kid bid did forbid grid hid invalid lid Madrid pyramid rid skid slid squid

Kill (see **Fill**)

Killer caterpillar chiller distiller driller filler instiller pillar shriller spiller swiller thriller tiller

Killing (see **Willing**)

Kin aspirin been begin Berlin bin chagrin chin discipline feminine fin genuine gin grin harlequin heroine in inn mandolin mannequin masculine moccasin origin pin saccharine shin sin skin spin thick-and-thin thin tin twin violin win within

Kind behind bind blind find grind hind humankind

mastermind mind remind signed unkind unwind wind wined

Kindle dwindle rekindle spindle swindle

King anything bring cling ding evening everything fling ring sing sling spring sting string swing thing wing wring (add "ing" to "action" words, i.e., run(ning), etc.)

Kingdom (see **Dumb**)

Kinky blinky dinky pinky slinky stinky

Kiss abyss amiss analysis armistice carcass cowardice dismiss emphasis hiss hypothesis miss nemesis office prejudice Swiss synthesis this

Kissing dismissing 'dissing hissing missing reminiscing

Kit befit bit fit 'git grit knit hit idiot it lit nit-wit pit quit sit twit unfit wit zit

Kitten bitten Briton mitten smitten written (see *in*)

Kitty city committee ditty gritty pity pretty self-pity witty

Knee (see **Be**)

Knew adieu anew avenue barbecue bayou chew choo-choo cue curfew debut dew due ensue ewe few guru honeydew hue I.O.U. imbue ingénue interview Jew lieu new Nehru overdue pee-ewe pew preview pursue renew residue revenue review spew subdue sue undue view yew you (see *do*)

Knight (see **Light**)

Knife afterlife jackknife life strife wife

Knob blob bob cob fob gob hob hobnob job lob mob nob rob slob snob sob swab throb

Knock (see **Clock**)

Knot apricot blot Camelot clot cot cybot dot forget-me-not forgot fought gavotte got hot hot-shot jot lot not plot pot robot rot shot slingshot somewhat spot squat swat tot trot watt what yacht

Know afro although banjo beau below bestow blow bow buffalo bungalow calico crossbow crow depot doe domino dough embryo escrow Eskimo flow foe forgo fro gazebo gigolo glow go grow heigh ho ho-ho hobo hoe incognito indigo Joe long-ago low Mexico mistletoe mow no oboe oh outgrow overflow overgrow overthrow owe Pinocchio pistachio plateau quo rainbow ratio roe row sew slow snow so Soho status quo stow studio tally-ho though throw tiptoe to-and-fro toe Tokyo tow tremolo undergo undertow vertigo woe yo yo-yo

Knowledge acknowledge college (see *ledge*)

Known alone atone backbone baritone blown bone chaperone clone condone cone cornerstone cyclone Dictaphone flown full-blown full-grown gramophone grindstone groan grown headstone loan lone microphone milestone moan monotone mown overgrown overthrown own phone postpone prone saxophone sewn shown stone telephone thrown tone trombone unknown xylophone zone

Knuckle arbuckle buckle chuckle honeysuckle suckle

Koran an ban can can-can Dan fan Iran man Nan plan Tehran

Kosher so sure (see *her*)

L

Lab   blab cab crab dab drab gab grab jab nab scab slab stab tab

Label   (see **Able**)

Labor   belabor neighbor saber

Lack   almanac attack back black bric-a-brac Cadillac cardiac clickety-clack egomaniac feedback hack Hackensack haystack jack kleptomaniac knack maniac pack plaque Pontiac prozac quack rack sack shack slack snack stack tack track whack yak zodiac

Lad   (see **Mad**)

Lamp   amp camp champ clamp cramp damp ramp stamp vamp

Land   and band brand canned command contraband demand expand fanned grand hand panned planned reprimand Rio Grande sand stand

Lane   (see **Rain**)

Large   barge charge discharge enlarge

Lark   aardvark arc ark bark dark embark hark mark narc park patriarch remark shark spark stark

Laser   appraiser blazer gazer maser phaser praiser razor stargazer

Lash   ash balderdash bash brash cash clash crash

dash flash gnash rash rehash slash smash splash stash thrash trash

Last   aghast blast cast classed contrast fast flabbergast forecast gassed mast outlast overcast passed past vast

Late   (see **Ate**)

Latin   battin' cattin' fatten flatten Manhattan paten Patton

Latitude   attitude gratitude platitude

Laugh   calf carafe epitaph giraffe graph paragraph phonograph photograph polygraph riffraff staff telegraph

Laughter   after grafter hereafter rafter thereafter

Lawn   (see **Dawn**)

Lazy   crazy daisy hazy

Lead   ahead bed bedspread bread bred coed dead dread fed figurehead fled flowerbed fountainhead gingerbread head inbred led misled misread overfed read red riverbed said shed shred sled sped spread thoroughbred thread underfed unthread wed

Leaf   beef belief brief chief disbelief grief relief thief

League   fatigue intrigue

Leak   beak bleak creek eek freak meek reek seek speak tweak weak week

Lean   (see **Mean**)

Leap barkeep cheep creep deep heap keep peep reap seep sheep sleep steep sweep weep

Learn adjourn burn churn concern discern earn fern intern kern overturn return sojourn spurn stern taciturn turn urn yearn

Leash quiche unleash

Least beast ceased creased deceased east feast pieced priest yeast

Leather altogether feather Heather tether together weather whether (see *her*)

Leave achieve believe bereave conceive disbelieve eve grieve heave perceive receive relieve reprieve retrieve sleeve weave

Lecture architecture conjecture

Ledge allege dredge edge fledge hedge privilege sacrilege sledge wedge

Left deft theft

Legal beagle eagle illegal regal sea gull

Leisure seizure

Lend (see **Friend**)

Length strength

Less access address baroness bashfulness bitterness bless caress chess cleverness cloudiness compress confess craziness deadliness depress digress distress dizziness dress duress eagerness easiness eeriness emptiness excess

express finesse foolishness ghostliness guess
happiness haziness homelessness idleness
impress joyfulness joylessness laziness
limitless Loch Ness lustfulness mess
nervousness obsess openness oppress
outrageousness penniless playfulness possess
press profess progress queasiness recess
regress repossess repress rockiness seediness
shallowness silkiness sleaziness sleepiness
sneakiness SOS spaciousness spitefulness
stress success suppress thoughtfulness
transgress uselessness viciousness willingness
wishfulness worldliness yes youthfulness

Let (see **Met**)

Letter better debtor getter setter sweater wetter

Level bedevil bevel devil dishevel level revel

Lewd (see **Feud**)

Liar amplifier beautifier briar buyer crier cryer drier
dryer flier friar higher mystifier occupier prior
simplifier slyer supplier testifier (see *fire*)

Liberty (see **Be**)

Librarian (see **Vegetarian**)

Lick arithmetic arsenic brick candlestick candlewick
Catholic chick click flick heartsick hick kick
limerick love-sick lunatic maverick nick pick
sick slick stick thick tic tick wick

Lid bid did forbid grid hid invalid kid Madrid

pyramid rid skid slid squid

Lie alibi amplify banzai barfly butterfly buy by bye
certify clarify crucify cry defy deify deny die
dignify diversify dragonfly drive-by dry dye eye
firefly fly fry glorify gratify guy high horrify I
identify imply July justify lullaby modify my
mystify notify passerby pie pry qualify rely rye
satisfy sci-fi shy sigh signify simplify sky sly
specify spry spy terrify testify thigh tie try
underlie verify why

Lied (see **Bride**)

Lies advertise advise analyze apologize arise
authorize baptize capitalize capsize
characterize comprise compromise criticize
demise deputize despise devise dies disguise
economize emphasize enterprise epitomize
eulogize excise exercise exorcise eyes
familiarize fertilize flies generalize hypnotize
idealize idolize immortalize improvise italicize
legalize materialize memorize merchandise
minimize neutralize ostracize paralyze
patronize penalize personalize philosophize
plagiarize prize rationalize realize recognize
reprise revise rise satirize scandalize scrutinize
size socialize specialize spies sterilize
stigmatize subsidize summarize sunrise
supervise surmise surprise sympathize terrorize
theorize thighs ties tranquilize utilize verbalize

visualize vocalize wise

Life afterlife jackknife knife strive wife

Lift drift gift shift spendthrift swift thrift

Light appetite bite blight bright byte contrite copyright daylight delight despite dynamite excite Fahrenheit fight flight fright headlight height ignite invite kite knight midnight might moonlight night outright parasite plight polite quite recite reunite right satellite sight site sleight slight spite starlight sunlight tight trite twilight unite white write

Like bike hike mike spike strike tyke

Liking biking disliking spiking striking Viking

Lily Billy Chile Chili chilly dilly filly frilly hillbilly hilly Philly Piccadilly piccalilli shrilly silly willy-nilly

Limb brim dim grim gym hymn pseudonym skim slim swim trim whim

Limber timber timbre

Lime climb crime dime I'm pantomime prime rhyme slime summertime thyme time

Limp blimp gimp pimp shrimp skimp wimp

Line (see **Fine**)

Lingo bingo dingo flamingo gringo jingo (see *glow*)

Lion buyin' cryin' dandelion denyin' dyin' lyin' Orion Ryan sighin' tryin' Zion (see *in*)

List (see **Mist**)

Listen christen dissin' glisten hissin' kissin' missin'

Live affirmative alternative argumentative combative
competitive consecutive conservative definitive
expletive figurative forgive fugitive give
informative intuitive lucrative narrative
negative positive primitive prohibitive
provocative relative representative sensitive
talkative tentative

Livid vivid

Lizard blizzard gizzard scissored wizard

Load (see **Road**)

Loaf oaf

Loan (see **Lone**)

Lobster mobster

Local focal vocal yokel

Lock Bangkok beanstalk boondock clock cock
cornstalk crock deadlock defrock dock flintlock
flock frock gawk gridlock hawk hock J.S. Bach
jock knock Little Rock livestock mock Mohawk
padlock peacock rock shock sidewalk small talk
smock sock squawk stalk stock talk tomahawk
unlock walk wok

Locket docket hocket pocket rocket socket sprocket
(see *it*)

Lodge dislodge dodge hodgepodge lodge

Loft aloft oft soft

London undone (see *done*)

Lone alone atone backbone baritone blown bone chaperone clone condone cone cornerstone cyclone Dictaphone flown full-blown full-grown gramophone grindstone groan grown headstone known loan microphone milestone moan monotone mown overgrown overthrown own phone postpone prone saxophone sewn shown stone telephone thrown tone trombone unknown xylophone zone

Loner condoner donor groaner honer known 'er loan 'er loaner moaner owner phone 'er toner

Long along belong bong ding-dong gong Hong Kong Ping-Pong prong song strong throng wrong

Longing belonging prolonging wronging

Look book brook cook crook hook mistook nook outlook rook shook took undertook

Looking booking cooking hooking rooking

Loon (see **Moon**)

Loose caboose goose moose noose papoose recluse spruce truce vamoose

Lord aboard accord afford award board bored ford harpsichord hoard overboard poured reward shuffleboard soared sword ward

Los Angeles exodus helluva mess man jealous romances us scandalous unanimous unscramble us upper crust

L

Lose blues booze bruise choose cruise news ooze snooze whose

Loss across albatross boss cross double-cross floss gloss moss rhinoceros sauce toss

Lost bossed cost crossed exhaust flossed frost holocaust Pentecost tossed

Lot (see **Hot**)

Lottery pottery watery

Loud allowed aloud cloud crowd enshroud plowed proud shroud thundercloud

Louder chowder powder prouder (see *her*)

Lounge scrounge

Love above dove glove ladylove mourning dove of shove turtle dove

Lover cover discover hover recover rediscover shover undercover (see *her*)

Low (see **Blow**)

Loyal broil coil foil oil recoil royal spoil toil turmoil

Loyalty royalty (see *be*)

Luck amuck buck chuck cluck deduct duck horror-struck muck pluck potluck puck struck suck truck tuck

Lucky ducky Kentucky unlucky

Lumber cucumber cumber encumber number slumber umber

Lump bump chump clump dump hump jump plump rump slump stump thump trump ump

L

Lunar communer crooner harpooner lampooner
pruner schooner sooner spooner tuner

Lunch brunch bunch crunch hunch munch punch
scrunch

Lure (see **Cure**)

Lust adjust August bust crust disgust distrust
encrust entrust gust just mistrust must robust
rust thrust trust unjust

Luxury (see Be)

Lynch cinch flinch inch pinch

Lyrical empirical miracle satirical

madonna
wanna

main
detain

M

Machine (see **Mean**)

Machinery beanery greenery scenery

Mad ad add bad Brad cad Chad clad Dad egad fad glad grad had lad nomad pad plaid sad shad Trinidad

Made afraid aid arcade barricade blade blockade braid brayed brigade centigrade charade crusade degrade dismayed dissuade downgrade escapade evade fade grade grenade hayed invade laid lemonade maid masquerade paid parade persuade played promenade raid renegade serenade shade spade stockade suede tirade trade

Madonna belladonna Donna iguana prima donna wanna

Magic tragic (see *tick*)

Magician (see *tradition*)

Mail (see **Ale**)

Main abstain again airplane arraign ascertain attain brain Cain campaign cane chain champagne cocaine complain contain crane detain disdain domain drain entertain explain feign gain grain humane hurricane hydroplane insane lane Maine maintain mane migraine obtain ordain pain pane pertain plain plane profane propane rain refrain reign rein remain sane slain Spain sprain stain strain sustain train vain vane vein wane windowpane

Major   cager pager stager wager

Make   ache bake brake break cake fake flake forsake headache heartache keepsake mistake opaque quake rake sake shake snake stake steak take wake

Male   (see **Ale**)

Malevolent   benevolent

Malice   Alice chalice Dallas palace phallus

Mall   all ball bawl brawl call crawl doll drawl fall gall haul install maul Montreal nightfall overhaul parasol pitfall protocol rainfall scrawl shawl small snowfall sprawl stall tall thrall wall waterfall y'all

Malt   assault cobalt exalt fault halt salt somersault vault

Mamma   Bahama comma Dalai Lama drama llama melodrama pajama Yokohama

Man   ban can can-can Dan fan Iran Nan plan ran Tehran

Maneuver   Hoover mover prover remover Vancouver

Manic   (see **Volcanic**)

Manor   banner canner fanner manner planner

M

scanner spanner tanner

Manual annual

Many any Benny Jenny penny

Map cap chap clap flap gap handicap lap mishap nap rap sap scrap slap snap strap tap trap wrap zap

Maple papal staple

March arch parch starch

Mark aardvark arc ark bark dark embark hark lark narc park patriarch remark shark spark stark

Marquee malarkey marquis oligarchy patriarchy

Marriage carriage disparage miscarriage

Marry carry hairy hari-kari miscarry parry vary (see *cherry*)

Marrying carrying

Marsh harsh

Martyr barter Carter charter darter garter smarter starter tarter

Mash ash balderdash bash brash cash clash crash dash flash gnash lash rash rehash slash smash splash stash thrash trash

Mask ask bask cask flask task

Match attach batch catch detach dispatch hatch latch patch scratch snatch

Mate (see **Ate**)

M

Material   cereal immaterial managerial ministerial serial

Math   aftermath bath homeopath path psychopath sociopath wrath

Matrimony   acrimony alimony baloney bony crony macaroni patrimony phony pony sanctimony stony testimony Tony

May   (see **Say**)

Maybe   baby (see *be*)

Mayor   betrayer conveyor grayer layer payer player portrayer prayer slayer soothsayer sprayer stayer surveyor

M

Me   (see **Be**)

Mean   bean between caffeine canteen chlorine clean codeine Colleen convene cuisine dean demean evergreen Florentine foreseen gasoline Gene green guillotine Halloween in-between intervene kerosene lean lien machine marine mezzanine Nazarene nectarine nicotine obscene preen quarantine queen ravine routine sardine scene seen serene spleen submarine tambourine tangerine teen thirteen (etc.) Vaseline velveteen wintergreen wolverine

Meant   (see **Bent**)

Measure   displeasure pleasure treasure

Meat   (see **Meet**)

Mechanical   botanical manacle tyrannical

Medal   meddle pedal peddle

Medium   tedium (see *some*)

Meek   beak bleak creek eek freak leak reek seek speak tweak weak week

Meet   athlete beat beet bittersweet bleat cheat compete complete conceit concrete deceit defeat delete deplete discreet discrete eat elite feat feet fleet greet heat incomplete indiscreet meat meet mistreat neat obsolete parakeet receipt repeat retreat seat sheet sleet street suite sweet treat wheat

Melancholy   collie dolly finale folly golly jolly Molly Polly tamale trolley volley

Mellow   bellow cello fellow hello Othello yellow

Melodic   episodic methodic periodic

Melody   (see **Be**)

Melt   belt Celt dealt felt heartfelt pelt welt

Member   December dismember ember November remember September

Memo   demo

Memory   (see **Be**)

Men   amen citizen den fen hen hydrogen Ken oxygen pen regimen specimen ten then yen zen

Menace   tennis

M

Mend (see **Friend**)

Menial congenial

Mental accidental coincidental complemental
continental dental departmental detrimental
experimental fundamental gentle
governmental incidental intercontinental lentil
monumental Oriental parental regimental
rental rudimental sentimental supplemental
temperamental

Mess access address baroness bashfulness
bitterness bless caress chess cleverness
cloudiness compress confess craziness
deadliness depress digress distress dizziness
dress duress eagerness easiness eeriness
emptiness excess express finesse foolishness
ghostliness guess happiness haziness
homelessness idleness impress joyfulness
joylessness laziness less limitless Loch Ness
lustfulness nervousness obsess openness
oppress outrageousness penniless playfulness
possess press profess progress queasiness
recess regress repossess repress rockiness
seediness shallowness silkiness sleaziness
sleepiness sneakiness SOS spaciousness
spitefulness stress success suppress
thoughtfulness transgress uselessness
viciousness willingness wishfulness
worldliness yes youthfulness

M

Messiah Jeremiah Maya papaya

Messy dressy

Met alphabet bayonet bet brunette cabinet cadet
cigarette clarinet cornet corvette debt duet
epithet etiquette forget fret gazette get jet
Joliet Juliet let luncheonette marionette net
omelet pet quartet regret roulette set
silhouette Somerset sunset sweat threat Tibet
toilette upset vet 'vette violet wet yet

Metal kettle mettle petal resettle settle

Mice advice concise device dice entice ice lice nice
paradise precise price rice sacrifice spice splice
suffice thrice twice vice

Middle diddle fiddle griddle riddle twiddle

Midget digit fidget widget

Might (see **Night**)

Mild child dialed piled smiled wild

Mile (see **Smile**)

Military (see **Ordinary**)

Milk bilk ilk silk

Million billion Brazilian Maximillian pavilion
reptilian trillion zillion

Millionaire (see **Air**)

Mind behind bind blind find grind hind humankind
kind mastermind remind signed unkind unwind
wind wined

Mine align asinine assign benign combine
concubine confine consign decline define
design dine divine entwine feline fine incline
line malign nine outshine pine porcupine
recline refine resign Rhine shine shrine sign
spine stein swine twine underline undermine
vine whine wine

Mingle intermingle jingle Kris Kringle shingle single
tingle

Miniature (see **Pure**)

Minister administer sinister

Minor cosigner designer diner eyeliner finer liner
miner refiner shiner signer

Mint flint hint lint spearmint peppermint print splint
sprint squint tint

Minus sinus (see *us*)

Minute spinet (see *it*)

Miracle empirical lyrical satirical

Mirage barrage camouflage garage entourage

Mirror cheerer clearer dearer hearer jeerer nearer
queerer severer sneerer spearer

Misery (see **Be**)

Miss abyss amiss analysis armistice bliss carcass
cowardice 'diss dismiss emphasis hiss
hypothesis kiss nemesis office prejudice Swiss
synthesis this

Missile bristle dismissal gristle missal sisal thistle whistle

Mission (see **Tradition**)

Mist accompanist analyst anarchist anthropologist archeologist assist biologist Calvinist capitalist coexist communist consist cyst desist dismissed egoist essayist evangelist exist exorcist fatalist gist hissed humanist humorist idealist imperialist insist journalist kissed list lobbyist Methodist missed moralist motorist nationalist novelist organist perfectionist pharmacist pianist plagiarist psychologist romanticist satirist sentimentalist socialist soloist specialist strategist terrorist theologist theorist twist ventriloquist vocalist wrist

Mistake ache bake brake break cake fake flake forsake headache heartache keepsake make opaque quake rake shake snake stake steak take wake

Mistaken achin' bacon forsaken Jamaican makin' overtaken shaken undertaken taken unshaken waken

Mister assister blister magister resister sister twister (see *her*)

Misty Christie Corpus Christi twisty (see *tea*)

Mitt befit bit fit 'git grit kit knit hit it lit nit-wit pit quit sit twit unfit ultimate wit zit

Mix acrobatics bics crucifix fiddlesticks fix kicks licks mathematics nix picks politics six sticks Styx ticks transfix tricks wicks

Mixer elixir fixer (see *her*)

Mixture fixture

Moan alone atone backbone baritone blown bone chaperone clone condone cone cornerstone cyclone Dictaphone flown full-blown full-grown gramophone grindstone groan grown headstone known loan lone microphone milestone monotone mown overgrown overthrown own phone postpone prone saxophone sewn shown stone telephone thrown tone trombone unknown xylophone zone

Mob blob bob cob fob gob hob hobnob job knob lob nob rob slob snob sob swab throb

Mobster lobster

Mock (see **Shock**)

Model coddle remodel swaddle toddle twaddle waddle

Mogul ogle

Moist hoist joist rejoiced voiced

Molester Chester contester fester investor jester Lester pester protester semester sequester tester Westchester Winchester

M

Mom aplomb bomb calm embalm Guam palm psalm qualm

Monday one day Sunday (see *day*)

Money bunny funny honey runny sunny

Monk bunk chunk clunk cyberpunk drunk dunk flunk funk hunk junk plunk punk shrunk skunk slunk spunk stunk sunk trunk

Monkey chunky flunky funky spunky

Mood brood clued conclude crude dude exclude food glued include intrude misconstrued mood preclude prude rude seclude shrewd wooed

Moon afternoon baboon balloon bassoon boon buffoon cartoon cocoon coon croon goon harpoon harvest moon honeymoon lagoon lampoon loon maroon monsoon noon platoon prune raccoon saloon Saskatoon soon spittoon swoon tycoon typhoon (see *tune*)

Moose caboose goose loose noose papoose recluse spruce truce vamoose

Mop (see **Drop**)

Moral aural choral floral immoral laurel oral

More (see **Door**)

Mortal chortle immortal portal

Most boast coast foremost furthermost ghost host innermost post roast toast whipping post

Mother another brother other smother

M

Motion   commotion emotion locomotion lotion
notion ocean potion promotion

Motive   emotive locomotive

Motto   blotto grotto legato staccato

Mound   (see **Found**)

Mountain   countin' fountain

Mourn   adorn airborne born Cape Horn Capricorn
forlorn forsworn horn lovelorn Matterhorn
morn popcorn scorn seaborne stillborn sworn
unicorn warn worn

Mouse   blouse douse grouse house louse madhouse
outhouse penthouse slaughterhouse souse
spouse

Move   approve behoove disapprove disprove groove
improve prove remove

Movie   groovy

Mow   (see **Blow**)

Much   clutch crutch Dutch hutch inasmuch retouch
such touch

Muck   (see **Truck**)

Mud   blood bud cud dud flood mud scud spud stud
thud

Muffin   puffin ragamuffin stuffin' toughen

Muffle   duffle ruffle scuffle shuffle truffle

Mule   molecule ridicule vestibule Yule

M

Mumble bumble crumble fumble grumble humble jumble mumble rumble stumble tumble

Mural extramural intramural neural plural rural

Murder girder herder

Muscle bustle corpuscle hustle mussel rustle tussle

Music arsenic brick candlestick Catholic chick click flick heartsick hick kick lick limerick love-sick maverick nick pick sick slick stick thick tic tick

Musician (see **Tradition**)

Muss (see **Us**)

Must adjust August bust crust disgust distrust encrust entrust gust just lust mistrust robust rust thrust trust unjust

M

Mustard custard

My (see **Cry**)

Mystery history

N

Nail (see **Ale**)

Name acclaim aim became blame came claim exclaim fame flame frame game inflame lame maim proclaim same shame tame

Narc aardvark arc ark bark dark embark hark lark mark park patriarch remark shark spark stark

Narcotic chaotic erotic exotic hypnotic idiotic macrobiotic quixotic

Narrate (see **Ate**)

Narrow arrow barrow harrow marrow sparrow tarot

National international irrational rational passional

Native accumulative appreciative authoritative communicative creative decorative generative hesitative imitative innovative investigative operative vindictive

Naughty dotty knotty manicotti spotty

Near adhere appear atmosphere auctioneer beer bombardier career cashier cavalier chandelier cheer clear dear deer disappear ear engineer fear financier frontier gear hear hemisphere here insincere interfere jeer lavaliere leer mere mountaineer overhear overseer peer persevere pioneer queer racketeer reappear rear revere seer severe shear sheer sincere smear sneer spear sphere stratosphere tear veneer volunteer year

Neat (see **Meet**)

Necessary (see **Ordinary**)

Neck check Czech deck fleck heck peck Quebec speck trek wreck

Need agreed breed centipede concede creed deed exceed feed greed heed inbreed knead lead mislead precede proceed read recede reed secede seed speed stampede succeed Swede tweed weed

Neglect (see **Effect**)

Neighbor belabor labor saber

Neither breather either

Neon eon peon (see *dawn*)

Nerve conserve curve deserve observe preserve reserve serve swerve

Nest (see **Best**)

Never clever endeavor ever forever however lever sever whatever whenever wherever whoever

New adieu anew avenue barbecue bayou chew choo-choo cue curfew debut dew due ensue ewe few guru honeydew hue I.O.U. imbue ingénue interview Jew knew ieu new Nehru overdue pee-ewe pew preview pursue renew residue revenue review spew subdue sue undue view yew you (see *do*)

New York   cork fork pitchfork pork stork torque uncork

Next   context flexed pretext text

Nibble   dribble kibble quibble scribble Sibyl

Nice   advice concise device dice entice ice lice mice paradise precise price rice sacrifice spice splice suffice thrice twice vice

Night   appetite bite blight bright byte contrite copyright daylight delight despite dynamite excite Fahrenheit fight flight fright headlight height ignite invite kite knight light midnight might moonlight outright parasite plight polite quite recite reunite right satellite sight site sleight slight spite starlight sunlight tight trite twilight unite white write

Nightmare   (see **Air**)

Nile   (see **Smile**)

Nirvana   Americana banana bandanna Diana Hannah Havana hosanna Indiana Louisiana Pollyanna Savannah Texarkana

No   afro although banjo beau below bestow blow bow buffalo bungalow calico crossbow crow depot doe domino dough embryo escrow Eskimo flow foe forgo fro gazebo gigolo glow go grow heigh-ho ho-ho hobo hoe incognito indigo Joe know long ago low Mexico mistletoe mow oboe oh outgrow overflow overgrow overthrow owe Pinocchio pistachio plateau quo

N

rainbow ratio roe row sew slow snow so Soho
status quo stow studio tally-ho though throw
tiptoe to-and-fro toe Tokyo tow tremolo
undergo undertow vertigo woe yo yo-yo

Nobody body embody gaudy lawdy shoddy
somebody toddy

Nocturnal colonel eternal external fraternal infernal
internal journal kernel maternal paternal

Nod abroad applaud awed broad clod cod defraud
façade fraud God guffawed Izod odd pod prod
promenade quad rod roughshod shod sod
squad trod wad

Noise poise

None anyone begun bun comparison done everyone
fun Galveston gun hon Hun jettison nun
oblivion one outdone outrun overdone overrun
phenomenon pun run shun simpleton skeleton
son stun sun ton unison venison won

Noodle boodle caboodle doodle feudal poodle
Yankee Doodle

Noon afternoon baboon balloon bassoon boon
buffoon cartoon cocoon coon croon goon
harpoon harvest moon honeymoon lagoon
lampoon loon maroon monsoon moon platoon
prune raccoon saloon Saskatoon soon spittoon
swoon tycoon typhoon (see *tune*)

Noose caboose goose loose moose papoose recluse
spruce truce vamoose

Normal abnormal formal informal

North forth fourth henceforth

Not apricot blot Camelot clot cot cybot dot forget-me-not forgot fought gavotte got hot hot-shot jot knot lot plot pot robot rot shot slingshot somewhat spot squat swat tot trot watt what yacht

Notate rotate (see *ate*)

Notch blotch botch crotch debauch hopscotch Scotch wristwatch

Note afloat antidote bloat boat coat connote denote dote float footnote gloat goat misquote moat oat overcoat promote quote remote riverboat rote smote throat tote underwrote vote wrote

Notorious (see **Us**)

Novel grovel hovel

Now allow avow bough bow brow chow cow disavow endow frau how kowtow ow plough plow row slough somehow sow thou vow wow

Nude (see **Feud**)

Numb album aquarium auditorium become bum burdensome Christendom come cranium crematorium crumb curriculum dumb drum emporium fee-fi-fo-fum glum gum gymnasium hum kettledrum kingdom martyrdom maximum meddlesome medium millennium

minimum mum museum opium overcome
pendulum petroleum platinum plum premium
quarrelsome radium random rum sanitarium
scum slum some strum succumb sum swum
tedium thumb Tom Thumb Tweedledum
uranium worrisome yum

Number cucumber cumber encumber lumber
slumber umber

Nurse adverse converse curse disburse disperse
diverse hearse immerse intersperse inverse
purse rehearse reverse terse transverse traverse
universe verse worse

Nursery anniversary cursory

Nurture searcher

Nutty putty smutty

O

Oaf loaf

Oath both growth loath overgrowth undergrowth

Obey (see **Say**)

Object (see **Defect**)

Objection (see **Rejection**)

Obscenity amenity identity serenity

Observe conserve curve deserve nerve preserve
    reserve serve swerve

Occasion abrasion dissuasion equation evasion
    invasion persuasion

Ocean commotion emotion locomotion lotion
    motion notion potion promotion

Odd abroad applaud awed broad clod cod defraud
    façade fraud God guffawed Izod nod pod prod
    promenade quad rod roughshod shod sod
    squad trod wad

Ode (see **Road**)

Odor exploder goader loader

Of above dove glove ladylove love mourning dove
    shove turtle dove

Off cough scoff trough

Offensive apprehensive comprehensive defensive
    expensive extensive incomprehensive
    inexpensive intensive pensive

Offer coffer cougher scoffer

Often coffin coughin' soften

Office abyss amiss analysis armistice bliss carcass
cowardice 'diss dismiss emphasis hiss
hypothesis kiss miss nemesis prejudice Swiss
synthesis this

Ogle mogul

Oh (see **So**)

Oil broil coil foil loyal recoil royal spoil toil turmoil

Old behold blindfold bold centerfold cold fold
foothold foretold gold hold household
marigold mold retold scold sold told uphold
withhold

On Amazon autobahn Babylon bonbon Bonn brawn
chiffon con dawn drawn echelon fawn gone
lawn neon pawn pentagon silicon swan
undergone upon wan woebegone wonton yawn

Once bunts dunce fronts

One anyone begun bun comparison done everyone
fun Galveston gun hon Hun jettison none nun
oblivion outdone outrun overdone overrun
phenomenon pun run shun simpleton skeleton
son stun sun ton unison venison won

Only lonely

Ooze blues booze bruise choose cruise lose news
ooze snooze whose

Opt adopt copped flopped mopped popped stopped

Or (see **Door**)

Orchard tortured

Order boarder border disorder hoarder recorder

Ordinary adversary airy arbitrary beneficiary berry
bury canary capillary cautionary cherry
commentary culinary customary dairy
dictionary dietary dignitary disciplinary
discretionary evolutionary extraordinary fairy
February ferry functionary hairy hereditary
honorary imaginary incendiary intermediary
January Jerry legendary legionary literary
luminary Mary mercenary military momentary
monetary mortuary nary necessary obituary
Perry planetary prairie proprietary pulmonary
reactionary revolutionary sanctuary sanitary
scary secretary seminary sherry solitary
stationary temporary Terry Tipperary very
visionary vocabulary voluntary wary

Organ gorgon Morgan

Other another brother mother smother

Ouch couch crouch grouch pouch slouch vouch

Ounce announce bounce counts denounce mounts
pounce pronounce renounce trounce

Our devour flour hour scour (see *flower*)

Out about boy scout blow-out bout clout devout
doubt eke out flout gout lout pout roundabout
route scout shout snout spout sprout stout
tout trout wash-out worn-out

Outsider   chider cider decider divider glider insider low-rider provider rider slider spider wider

Oven   lovin' shovin' sloven

Over   clover Dover drover moreover rover

Overload   a la mode abode bode code corrode episode erode explode forebode goad load lode mode mowed lode ode road rode sowed toad unload

Overwhelm   elm helm realm whelm

Owe   (see **Blow**)

Owl   cowl foul fowl growl howl jowl prowl scowl waterfowl

Own   alone atone backbone baritone blown bone chaperone clone condone cone cornerstone cyclone Dictaphone flown full-blown full-grown gramophone grindstone groan grown headstone known loan lone microphone milestone moan monotone mown overgrown overthrown phone postpone prone saxophone sewn shown stone telephone thrown tone trombone unknown xylophone zone

Owner   condoner donor groaner honer known 'er loan 'er loaner loner moaner owner phone 'er toner

Ox   box chickenpox equinox fox mailbox orthodox paradox

Oxygen   amen citizen den fen hen hydrogen men Ken pen regimen specimen ten then yen zen

P

Pacific hieroglyphic horrific prolific scientific specific terrific

Pack almanac attack back black bric-a-brac Cadillac cardiac clickety-clack egomaniac feedback hack Hackensack haystack jack kleptomaniac knack lack maniac plaque Pontiac prozac quack rack sack shack slack snack stack tack track whack yak zodiac

Packet bracket jacket racket (see *it*)

Packing backing cracking hacking lacking ransacking smacking tracking whacking

Paddle saddle straddle

Page age cage gage rampage sage stage wage

Paid aid arcade afraid barricade blade blockade braid brayed brigade centigrade charade crusade degrade dismayed dissuade downgrade escapade evade fade grade grenade hayed invade laid lemonade made maid masquerade parade persuade played promenade raid renegade serenade shade spade stockade suede tirade trade

Pain abstain again airplane arraign ascertain attain brain Cain campaign cane chain champagne cocaine complain contain crane detain disdain

domain drain entertain explain feign gain grain
humane hurricane hydroplane insane lane
main Maine maintain mane migraine obtain
ordain pane pertain plain plane profane
propane rain refrain reign rein remain sane
slain Spain sprain stain strain sustain train
vain vane vein wane windowpane

Paint acquaint ain't complaint faint quaint restraint
saint taint 'tain't

Pair (see **Air**)

Pal canal chorale gal morale shall

Palace Alice chalice Dallas malice phallus

Panel channel flannel

Panic (see **Volcanic**)

Paper caper draper escaper raper scraper shaper
skyscraper taper (see *her*)

Parachute (see **Shoot**)

Parade (see **Afraid**)

Paradise advice concise device dice entice ice lice
mice nice precise price rice sacrifice spice
splice suffice thrice twice vice

Parent apparent grandparent transparent (see *ant*)

Park aardvark arc ark bark dark embark hark lark
mark narc patriarch remark shark spark stark

Parody (see **Be**)

Parole (see **Roll**)

Parrot carat carrot ferret merit tear it wear it (see *sit*)

Parted broken-hearted carted charted chicken-hearted cold-hearted darted departed fainthearted halfhearted hardhearted lion-hearted smarted started

Particle article nautical

Party arty hearty smarty tarty

Pass (see **Class**)

Passion ashen bashin' compassion fashion impassion

Past aghast blast cast classed contrast fast flabbergast forecast gassed last mast outlast overcast passed vast

Pastor blaster caster castor disaster faster flabbergaster forecaster master plaster postmaster taskmaster

Patch attach batch catch detach dispatch hatch latch match scratch snatch

Path aftermath bath homeopath math psychopath sociopath wrath

Pathetic aesthetic alphabetic apathetic apologetic arithmetic athletic cosmetic electromagnetic energetic frenetic genetic poetic sympathetic synthetic theoretic

Patrol (see **Roll**)

P

Pauper (see **Proper**)

Pause applause because cause clause claws gauze laws menopause Oz paws Santa Claus was

Pawn Amazon Babylon begone bonbon Bonn brawn chiffon con Don dawn drawn fawn gone hexagon John lawn lexicon octagon on Oregon pentagon silicon undergone upon withdrawn wanton yawn

Pay array bay betray bluejay bouquet bray clay day decay delay disarray dismay display eh? essay exposé fray gay gray hay hey holiday hooray José Kay lay matinee may moiré naysay negligée obey play portray protégé ray résumé ricochet risqué rosé say slay sleigh soufflé stay stray sway they toupee way weigh x-ray

Peace cease crease decease decrease fleece geese grease Greece increase lease mantelpiece masterpiece piece police release

P

Pearl curl earl girl hurl swirl twirl whirl

Pearly burly curly girlie squirrelly surly swirly

Peck check Czech deck fleck heck neck Quebec speck trek wreck

Pedal medal meddle peddle

Peep barkeep cheep creep deep heap keep leap reap seep sheep sleep steep sweep weep

Pen amen citizen den fen hen hydrogen Ken men oxygen regimen specimen ten then yen zen

Pencil prehensile stencil utensil

Penny any Benny Jenny many

People Steeple (see *pull*)

Perfect (see **Defect**)

Perfume assume consume costume exhume
   presume resume (see *room*)

Perish bearish cherish

Perjury surgery

Perky Albuquerque murky quirky turkey

Permission (see **Tradition**)

Persistent assistant consistent distant existent
   inconsistent insistent resistant subsistent

Persuasive dissuasive evasive invasive pervasive

Pervert (see **Hurt**)

Pest (see **Best**)

Pet alphabet bayonet bet brunette cabinet cadet
   cigarette clarinet cornet corvette debt duet
   forget fret gazette get jet Joliet Juliet let
   luncheonette marionette met net omelet pet
   quartet regret roulette set silhouette Somerset
   sunset sweat threat Tibet toilette upset vet
   'vette violet wet yet

Petty confetti jetty machete spaghetti sweaty

Phone alone atone backbone baritone blown bone
   chaperone clone condone cone cornerstone

cyclone Dictaphone flown full-blown full-grown gramophone grindstone groan grown headstone known loan lone microphone milestone moan monotone mown overgrown overthrown own phone postpone prone saxophone sewn shown stone telephone thrown tone trombone unknown xylophone zone

Phony acrimony alimony baloney bony crony macaroni matrimony patrimony pony sanctimony stony testimony Tony

Photo De Soto koto roto Toto

Pianist (see **Mist**)

Pick arithmetic arsenic brick candlestick candlewick Catholic chick click flick heartsick hick kick lick limerick love-sick lunatic maverick music nick sick slick stick thick tic tick wick

Picket cricket thicket ticket wicket (see *it*)

Pie (see **Cry**)

Piece cease crease decease decrease fleece geese grease Greece increase lease mantelpiece masterpiece peace police release

Pierce fierce

Pig big dig fig gig jig renege rig swig thingamajig twig wig

Pigeon religion widgeon

P

Pile (see **Smile**)

Pillage tillage village

Pillar caterpillar chiller distiller driller filler instiller
   killer shriller spiller swiller thriller tiller

Pillow armadillo billow peccadillo willow

Pimp blimp gimp limp shrimp skimp wimp

Pimple dimple simple

Pin (see **Been**)

Pinch cinch flinch inch lynch

Pink blink brink chink clink drink fink ink kink link
   mink rink shrink sink slink stink wink zinc

Pipe archetype gripe hype prototype ripe stereotype
   stripe swipe type wipe

Pistol crystal

Pitied prettied

Pity city committee ditty gritty kitty pretty self-pity
   witty

Pivot divot (see *it*)

Place ace base bass brace case chase commonplace
   debase disgrace displace embrace encase erase
   face grace lace mace misplace pace race
   replace space steeplechase trace unlace vase

Plague vague

Plan an ban can can-can Dan fan Iran man Nan ran
   Tehran

Plane (see **Pain**)

Planet gannet granite Janet pomegranate (see *it*)

Plant ant aunt can't chant decant enchant grant implant rant scant shan't slant transplant

Plastic bombastic drastic elastic enthusiastic fantastic gymnastic iconoclastic sarcastic scholastic spastic

Plate (see **Ate**)

Play (see **Say**)

Played (see **Afraid**)

Player betrayer conveyor grayer layer mayor payer portrayer prayer slayer soothsayer sprayer stayer surveyor

Pleasant omnipresent peasant pheasant present

Pleasure displeasure measure treasure

Plenty twenty

Plot (see **Hot**)

Plummet summit (see *it*)

Plump bump chump clump dump hump jump lump rump slump stump thump trump ump

Plunge lunge sponge

Plus (see **Us**)

Poem chrome chromosome comb dome foam gnome home honeycomb metronome Nome roam Rome tome

P

Poetic   aesthetic alphabetic apathetic apologetic arithmetic athletic cosmetic electromagnetic energetic frenetic genetic pathetic sympathetic synthetic theoretic

Point   anoint appoint counterpoint disappoint disjoint joint

Pole   (see **Roll**)

Police   cease crease decease decrease fleece geese grease Greece increase lease mantelpiece masterpiece peace piece release

Polish   (See **Abolish**)

Politician   (see **Tradition**)

Pollution   (see **Revolution**)

Pond   beyond blond bond correspond fond dawned respond spawned vagabond wand yawned

Ponder   condor conned 'er fonder launder squander wander yonder

Pony   acrimony alimony baloney bony crony macaroni matrimony patrimony phony sanctimony stony testimony Tony

Pooch   hooch mooch smooch

Poodle   boodle caboodle doodle feudal noodle Yankee Doodle

Pool   April fool cool drool fool ghoul Liverpool overrule rule school spool stool tool whirlpool

P

Poor amour boor contour detour moor paramour
   spoor tour (see *door*)

Pop (see **Drop**)

Pope (see **Hope**)

Porch scorch torch

Portion abortion contortion distortion extortion
   proportion

Posh (see **Wash**)

Post boast coast foremost furthermost ghost host
   innermost most roast toast whipping post

Pot apricot blot Camelot clot cot cybot dot forget-
   me-not forgot fought gavotte got hot hot-shot
   jot knot lot not plot robot rot shot slingshot
   somewhat spot squat swat tot trot watt what
   yacht

Potion commotion emotion locomotion lotion
   motion notion ocean promotion

Pound (see **Sound**)

Pour (see **Door**)

Powder chowder louder prouder (see *her*)

Power cauliflower cower deflower empower flower
   horsepower plower shower tower (see *our*)

Practical didactical tactical

Prairie (see **Ordinary**)

Prank bank blank clank crank dank drank flank frank

P

hank outrank plank rank sank shrank spank
stank tank thank yank

Prayer (see **Air**)

Prayer betrayer conveyor grayer layer mayor payer
player portrayer slayer soothsayer sprayer
stayer surveyor

Preach beach breach each impeach leech peach
reach screech speech teach

Preacher bleacher creature feature screecher
teacher

Precocious atrocious ferocious

Present omnipresent peasant pheasant pleasant

President resident (see *bent*)

Pressure fresher refresher thresher (see *sure*)

Pretender (see **Tender**)

Pretentious conscientious contentious

Pretty city committee ditty gritty kitty pity self-pity
witty

Price advice concise device dice entice ice lice mice
nice paradise precise rice sacrifice spice splice
suffice thrice twice vice

Pride beside bonafide bride collide confide
countryside decide defied died dignified divide
eyed fireside guide hide hillside homicide
inside lied outside override provide reside ride

side slide snide stride subdivide subside suicide tide tried wide yuletide

Priest   beast ceased creased deceased east feast least pieced yeast

Primate   climate (see *it, ate*)

Prime   climb crime dime I'm lime pantomime rhyme slime summertime thyme time

Prince   convince hints mints rinse since wince

Print   flint hint lint mint peppermint spearmint splint sprint squint tint

Prior   amplifier beautifier briar buyer crier cryer drier dryer flier friar higher mystifier occupier simplifier slyer supplier testifier (see *fire*)

Prison   arisen risen wizen (see *in*)

Privilege   allege dredge edge fledge hedge ledge privilege sacrilege sledge wedge

Prize   (see **Lies**)

Probe   disrobe globe Job robe strobe

Produce   (see **Use**)

Producer   reducer seducer transducer (see *sir*)

Profit   prophet (see *it*)

Progressive   aggressive depressive digressive excessive expressive impressive possessive regressive successive

Pronounce   announce bounce counts denounce

mounts ounce pounce renounce trounce

Proof aloof bulletproof goof hoof roof spoof
waterproof weatherproof

Proper bebopper bopper chopper copper cropper
dropper eavesdropper eyedropper grasshopper
hopper improper pauper popper sharecropper
shopper stopper swapper teenybopper topper
whopper (see *her*)

Prophet profit (see *it*)

Prostitution (see **Revolution**)

Protect (see **Defect**)

Protester Chester contester fester investor jester
Lester molester pester semester sequester
tester Westchester Winchester

Proud allowed aloud cloud crowd enshroud loud
plowed shroud thundercloud

Prove approve behoove disapprove disprove groove
improve move remove

Provoke (see **Joke**)

Prude brood clued conclude crude dude exclude
food glued include intrude misconstrued mood
preclude rude seclude shrewd wooed

Psalm aplomb bomb calm embalm Guam Mom
palm qualm

Psychosis diagnosis narcosis neurosis prognosis
psychosis

Pub Beelzebub bub club cub grub hub hubbub rub rub-a-dub-dub scrub shrub snub stub sub tub

Pucker bucker chucker clucker sapsucker seersucker sucker trucker (see *her*)

Puddle cuddle fuddle huddle muddle

Puke duke juke uke

Pull bull cock-and-bull do-able full wool (see *beautiful*)

Pulse convulse impulse repulse

Pumpkin bumpkin

Punch brunch bunch crunch hunch lunch munch scrunch

Puncture acupuncture conjuncture juncture

Punk bunk chunk clunk cyberpunk drunk dunk flunk funk hunk junk monk plunk shrunk skunk slunk spunk stunk sunk trunk

Punt affront blunt brunt bunt confront forefront front grunt hunt runt shunt stunt

Pup buttercup cup fed up hard-up pick-up pup suckup sup up

Pupil scruple

Puppy guppy yuppie

Pure allure armature assure brochure caricature cocksure cure demure endure ensure expenditure forfeiture immature impure

insecure insure liqueur literature lure manicure
mature miniature obscure overture pedicure
premature reassure secure signature sure
tablature temperature your

Purge (see **Verge**)

Push bush cush

Put afoot foot leadfoot pussyfoot tenderfoot

Puzzler guzzler muzzler

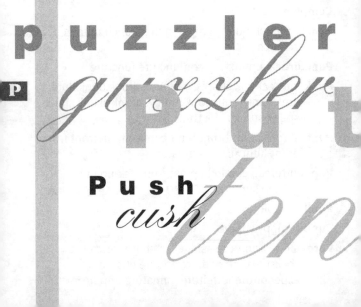

Q

Quaint acquaint ain't complaint faint paint restraint
saint taint 'tain't

Quake ache bake brake break cake fake flake forsake
headache heartache keepsake make mistake
opaque rake shake snake stake steak take wake

Quality (see **Be**)

Qualm aplomb bomb calm embalm Guam Mom
palm psalm

Quart abort assort cavort comfort contort court
davenport deport distort escort exhort export
extort fort import passport port report resort
retort short snort sort sport support thwart tort
transport wart

Queen bean between caffeine canteen chlorine clean
codeine Colleen convene cuisine dean demean
evergreen Florentine foreseen gasoline Gene
green guillotine Halloween in-between
intervene kerosene lean lien machine marine
mean mezzanine Nazarene nectarine nicotine
obscene preen quarantine ravine routine
sardine scene seen serene spleen submarine
tambourine tangerine teen thirteen (etc.)
Vaseline velveteen wintergreen wolverine

Queer (see **Near**)

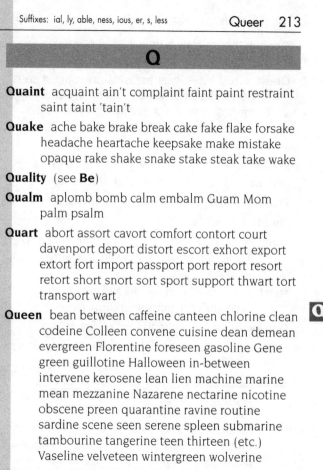

Prefixes: pre, re, in, con, de, mis

Quench bench clench drench French monkey wrench
stench trench wench wrench

Quest arrest attest best breast chest congest crest
detest digest divest double-breast infest ingest
interest invest jest manifest molest nest
protest request rest single-breast suggest test
vest

Quibble dribble kibble nibble scribble sibyl

Quicken chicken sicken stricken thicken (see *in*)

Quickly prickly sickly slickly stickly thickly

Quiet diet riot (see *it*)

Quip battleship chip clip dip drip equip flip grip gyp
hip lip nip rip scrip ship slip snip strip tip trip
whip zip

Quirk clerk handiwork irk jerk Kirk lurk murk
overwork perk quirk smirk Turk work

Quirky Albuquerque murky perky turkey

Quit befit bit fit 'git grit kit knit hit it lit mitt nit-wit
pit sit twit unfit ultimate wit zit

Quite appetite bite blight bright byte contrite
copyright daylight delight despite dynamite
excite Fahrenheit fight flight fright headlight
height ignite invite kite knight light midnight
might moonlight night outright parasite plight
polite recite reunite right satellite sight site
sleight slight spite starlight sunlight tight trite

Q

twilight unite white write

Quitter counterfeiter critter fitter fritter glitter litter
sitter transmitter twitter (see *her*)

Quiz biz fizz friz his is showbiz 'tis whiz

Quota Dakota iota Minnesota

Quote afloat antidote bloat boat coat connote
denote dote float footnote gloat goat misquote
moat note oat overcoat promote remote
riverboat rote smote throat tote underwrote
vote wrote

q u i z

whiz

q u i r k

work

q u e s t

q u o t e

suggest

vote

R

Rabble babble dabble scrabble

Racial facial glacial spatial

Racket bracket jacket packet (see *it*)

Rag bag brag drag flag gag hag lag mag nag sag shag slag snag stag swag tag wag

Raging aging caging gauging paging staging waging

Raid (see **Afraid**)

Rail (see **Ale**)

Rain abstain again airplane arraign ascertain attain brain Cain campaign cane chain champagne cocaine complain contain crane detain disdain domain drain entertain explain feign gain grain humane hurricane hydroplane insane lane main Maine maintain mane migraine obtain ordain pain pane pertain plain plane profane propane refrain reign rein remain sane slain Spain sprain stain strain sustain train vain vane vein wane windowpane

Rainbow (see **Blow**)

Raindrop chop cop crop drop eavesdrop flop hop lollipop mop plop pop prop shop stop swap tip-top whop

Rainy brainy grainy zany

Ramble amble gamble scramble shamble

Ran an ban can can-can Dan fan Iran Koran man
　　　Nan plan Tehran

Ranch avalanche branch

Range arrange change derange estrange exchange
　　　strange

Rank bank blank clank crank dank drank flank frank
　　　Hank outrank plank prank sank shrank spank
　　　stank tank thank yank

Rant (see **Ant**)

Rap cap chap clap flap gap handicap lap map
　　　mishap nap sap scrap slap snap strap tap trap
　　　wrap zap

Rape ape cape cityscape drape escape grape
　　　landscape seascape shape tape

Rapper capper clapper dapper flapper handicapper
　　　slapper snapper tapper whippersnapper
　　　wiretapper wrapper yapper

Rapture capture recapture (see *your*)

Rare (see **Air**)

Rate (see **Ate**)

Rational international irrational national passional

Rattle battle cattle chattel embattle prattle Seattle
　　　tattle

Ravage lavage savage scavage

R

Raw Arkansas awe bra caw claw draw flaw gnaw
guffaw hurrah jaw law Ma macaw nah overdraw
Pa paw saw seesaw shah slaw squaw straw
thaw withdraw

Razor appraiser blazer gazer laser maser phaser
praiser stargazer

Reach beach breach each impeach leech peach
preach screech speech teach

React (see **Act**)

Reaction (see **Action**)

Read agreed breed centipede concede creed deed
exceed feed greed heed inbreed knead lead
mislead need precede proceed recede secede
seed speed stampede succeed Swede tweed
weed

Read ahead bed bedspread bread bred coed dead
dread fed figurehead fled flowerbed
fountainhead gingerbread head inbred lead led
misled misread overfed red riverbed said shed
shred sled sped spread thoroughbred thread
underfed unthread wed

Realm elm helm overwhelm whelm

Rear (see **Near**)

Reason pleasin' season sneezin' squeezin' teasin'
wheezin' (see *son*)

Receipt (see **Meet**)

R

Receive achieve believe bereave conceive disbelieve eve grieve heave leave receive relieve reprieve retrieve sleeve weave

Recent decent indecent

Recital entitle title vital

Recognition (see **Tradition**)

Red (see **Said**)

Redemption exemption preemption

Refinery binary finery

Reflection (see **Rejection**)

Reflex complex decks duplex ex flex necks pecks Rolidex sex specs Tex unisex

Region collegian Norwegian

Regret alphabet bayonet bet brunette cabinet cadet cigarette clarinet cornet corvette debt duet epithet etiquette forget fret gazette get jet Joliet Juliet let luncheonette marionette met net omelet pet quartet roulette set silhouette Somerset sunset sweat threat Tibet toilette upset vet 'vette violet wet yet

Reject (see **Defect**)

Rejection affection bisection circumspection collection complexion connection correction defection deflection detection direction disaffection dissection ejection election erection imperfection infection inflection inspection intersection introspection objection perfection projection protection reflection resurrection retrospection section selection vivisection

Relax ax backs fax jacks lax max packs Saks sax slacks tax wax

Release cease crease decease decrease fleece geese grease Greece increase lease mantelpiece masterpiece peace piece police

Reliance alliance appliance compliance defiance reliance

Religion pigeon widgeon

Religious litigious prodigious sacrilegious

Remain (see **Rain**)

Remark aardvark arc ark bark dark embark hark lark mark narc park patriarch shark spark stark

Remember December dismember ember member November September

Reminiscing dismissing 'dissing hissing kissing missing

Remorse coarse course divorce endorse force horse Norse reinforce resource source

Remove approve behoove disapprove disprove groove improve move prove

Reno andantino bambino Filipino keno

Rent (see **Bent**)

Rental accidental coincidental complemental
      compliment continental dental departmental
      detrimental experimental fundamental gental
      governmental incidental intercontinental lentil
      mental monumental Oriental parental
      regimental rudimental sentimental
      supplemental temperamental

Repair (see **Air**)

Repeat (see **Meet**)

Resemble assemble dissemble tremble (see *bull*)

Resident president (see *bent*)

Resisted assisted cysted enlisted existed fisted
      insisted listed misted persisted subsisted
      twisted

Respect (see **Defect**)

Rest arrest attest best blessed breast Bucharest
      Budapest celeste chest congest contest crest
      detest digest divest dressed guessed guest
      infest ingest interest invest jest manifest
      messed molest nest pest protest request
      second-best suggest test unrest vest zest

Result adult catapult consult cult difficult exult
      insult occult

Retire (see **Fire**)

Return adjourn burn churn concern discern earn fern
      intern kern learn overturn sojourn spurn stern
      taciturn turn urn yearn

R

Reveal (see **Steal**)

Revenge avenge Stonehenge

Revolt bolt colt dolt jolt thunderbolt

Revolution absolution attribution constitution contribution destitution dilution dissolution distribution electrocution evolution execution institution pollution prosecution prostitution resolution retribution solution substitution

Revolve absolve devolve dissolve evolve involve solve

Revolver solver

Reward aboard accord afford award board bored ford harpsichord hoard lord overboard poured shuffleboard soared sword ward

Rhyme chime climb crime dime I'm lime mime pantomime prime slime summertime thyme time

Rib ad lib crib fib glib rib

Rich bewitch bitch ditch enrich glitch hitch pitch snitch stitch switch twitch which

Rid bid did forbid grid hid invalid lid Madrid pyramid skid slid squid

Riddle diddle fiddle griddle middle twiddle

Ride beside bonafide bride collide confide countryside decide defied died dignified divide eyed fireside guide hide hillside homicide

R

    inside lied outside override pride provide
    reside ride side slide snide stride subdivide
    subside suicide tide tried wide yuletide

Ridge abridge bridge fridge

Ridicule molecule mule ridicule vestibule Yule

Rifle Eiffel eyeful rifle stifle trifle

Rigid frigid

Ring anything bring cling ding evening everything
    fling king sing sling spring sting string swing
    thing wing wring (add "ing" to "action" words,
    i.e., run(ning), etc.)

Riot diet quiet (see *it*)

Rip (see **Trip**)

Ripe archetype gripe hype pipe prototype stereotype
    stripe swipe type wipe

Ripple cripple nipple triple

Rise (see **Lies**)

Risen arisen prison risen wizen (see *in*)

Rising advertising advising agonizing analyzing
    apologizing appetizing baptizing compromising
    criticizing despising devising disguising
    equalizing eulogizing evangelizing exercising
    generalizing harmonizing improvising
    jeopardizing memorizing mesmerizing
    minimizing modernizing organizing patronizing
    plagiarizing prizing realizing recognizing

R

revising scrutinizing sizing sterilizing subsidizing supervising surmising surprising sympathizing tantalizing terrorizing uprising utilizing visualizing vocalizing

Risk   asterisk brisk disk frisk whisk

Risky   frisky whiskey

Rival   arrival revival survival

River   deliver giver liver quiver shiver sliver (see *her*)

Roach   approach broach coach cockroach encroach poach reproach

Road   a la mode abode bode code corrode episode erode explode forebode goad load lode mode mowed lode ode overload rode sowed toad unload

Roam   chrome chromosome comb dome foam gnome home honeycomb metronome Nome poem Rome tome

Rob   blob bob cob fob gob hob hobnob job knob lob mob nob slob snob sob swab throb

Robber   clobber dauber jobber slobber swabber

Robe   disrobe globe Job probe strobe

Robust   (see **Trust**)

Rock   Bangkok beanstalk boondock clock cock cornstalk crock deadlock defrock dock flintlock flock frock gawk gridlock hawk hock J.S. Bach jock knock Little Rock livestock lock mock

R

Mohawk padlock peacock shock sidewalk small talk smock sock squawk stalk stock talk tomahawk unlock walk wok

Rocker balker blocker Knickerbocker knocker locker mocker shocker soccer stalker talker walker (see *her*)

Rocket docket hocket locket pocket socket sprocket (see *it*)

Rod abroad applaud awed broad clod cod defraud façade fraud God guffawed Izod nod odd pod prod promenade quad roughshod shod sod squad trod wad

Rode (see **Road**)

Roll bowl buttonhole cajole casserole coal control dole droll enroll goal hole loophole Maypole mole Old King Cole oriole parole patrol pole poll porthole role scroll tadpole toll troll whole

Roller bowler consoler controller molar polar solar stroller troller

Romance advance ants chance circumstance dance enhance extravagance finance France glance lance pants prance stance trance

Romantic antic Atlantic chromatic frantic gigantic pedantic transatlantic

Roof aloof bulletproof goof hoof proof spoof waterproof weatherproof

Rookie bookie cooky hooky lookee

Room bloom boom broom cloakroom doom entomb flume gloom groom tomb whom womb zoom

Roost boost

Rooster booster (see *her*)

Root (see **Shoot**)

Rope antelope cantaloupe cope dope elope envelope grope gyroscope hope horoscope kaleidoscope microscope mope pope scope slope soap stethoscope telescope

Rose arose chose close compose decompose depose disclose dispose doze enclose expose foreclose froze goes hose impose indispose interpose knows nose owes pose predispose presuppose prose recompose suppose those toes transpose woes

Rosy cozy dozy mosey posy

Rotate notate (see *ate*)

Rotten begotten cotton gotten forgotten

Rough bluff buff cuff duff enough fluff gruff huff muff powder puff scruff scuff snuff stuff tough

Rougher bluffer buffer duffer gruffer puffer suffer tougher

Round abound around astound background battleground bloodhound bound compound

R

confound downed dumbfound found ground hound impound merry-go-round mound pound profound renowned resound sound spellbound surround underground wound

Roar (see **Door**)

Routine (see **Mean**)

Row (see **Blow**)

Rowdy cloudy cum laude dowdy howdy

Royal broil coil foil loyal oil recoil spoil toil turmoil

Royalty loyalty (see *be*)

Rub Beelzebub bub club cub grub hub hubbub pub rub-a-dub-dub scrub shrub snub stub sub tub

Ruby booby

Rudder shudder udder

Rude brood clued conclude crude dude exclude food glued include intrude misconstrued mood preclude prude seclude shrewd wooed

Rule April fool cool drool fool ghoul Liverpool overrule pool school spool stool tool whirlpool

Ruler cooler drooler

Rum (see **Dumb**)

Rumor bloomer boomer consumer humor tumor

Run anyone begun bun comparison done everyone fun Galveston gun hon Hun jettison none nun oblivion one outdone outrun overdone overrun

R

phenomenon pun shun simpleton skeleton son stun sun ton unison venison won

Rung (see **Young**)

Runner gunner stunner

Rural extramural intramural mural neural plural

Rush blush brush crush flush gush lush mush plush slush thrush underbrush

Rust adjust August bust crust disgust distrust encrust entrust gust just lust mistrust must robust thrust trust unjust

R u n n e r
gunner

Rust

mistrust

rural

neural

S

Sack almanac attack back black bric-a-brac Cadillac cardiac clickety-clack egomaniac feedback hack Hackensack haystack jack kleptomaniac knack lack maniac pack plaque Pontiac prozac quack rack sack shack slack snack stack tack track whack yak zodiac

Sacrifice advice concise device dice entice ice lice mice nice paradise precise price rice spice splice suffice thrice twice vice

Sad ad add bad Brad cad Chad clad Dad egad fad glad grad had lad mad nomad pad plaid shad Trinidad

Saddle paddle straddle

Safe waif

Sag bag brag drag flag gag hag lag mag nag rag shag slag snag stag swag tag wag

Said ahead bed bedspread bread bred coed dead dread fed figurehead fled flowerbed fountainhead gingerbread head inbred lead led misled misread overfed read red riverbed shed shred sled sped spread thoroughbred thread underfed unthread wed

Sail (see **Ale**)

Sailor inhaler jailer sailor staler trailer wailer whaler

S

Saint　acquaint ain't complaint faint paint quaint restraint taint 'tain't

Salary　calorie gallery Mallory

Saloon　(see **Moon**)

Salt　assault cobalt exalt fault halt malt somersault vault

Salty　faulty malty

Same　acclaim aim became blame came claim exclaim fame flame frame game inflame lame maim name proclaim shame tame

Sample　ample example trample

Sand　and band brand canned command contraband demand expand fanned grand hand land panned planned reprimand Rio Grande stand

Sandal　candle dandle handle scandal vandal

Sandy　Andy brandy candy dandy handy randy

Sang　bang boomerang clang dang fang orangutan rang slang sprang

Sanity　Christianity humanity insanity profanity vanity

Sank　bank blank clank crank dank drank flank frank hank outrank plank prank rank shrank spank stank tank thank yank

Sappy　crappie happy nappy pappy scrappy slaphappy yappy

S

Sarcasm bioplasm chasm enthusiasm plasm spasm

Sarcastic bombastic drastic elastic enthusiastic fantastic gymnastic iconoclastic plastic scholastic spastic

Sat (see **At**)

Satisfactory factory refractory (see *story*)

Savage lavage ravage scavage

Save behave brave cave concave crave engrave forgave gave grave knave pave rave shave slave waive wave

Savior behavior misbehavior

Saw Arkansas awe bra caw claw draw flaw gnaw guffaw hurrah jaw law Ma macaw nah overdraw Pa paw raw seesaw shah slaw squaw straw thaw withdraw

Say array bay betray bluejay bouquet bray clay day decay delay disarray dismay display eh? essay exposé fray gay gray hay hey holiday hooray José Kay lay matinee may moiré naysay negligée obey pay play portray protégé ray résumé ricochet risqué rosé slay sleigh soufflé stay stray sway they toupee way weigh x-ray

Scald appalled bald

Scandal candle dandle handle sandal vandal

Scare (see **Air**)

Scarf barf snarf

S

Prefixes: pre, re, in, con, de, mis

Scary adversary airy arbitrary beneficiary berry bury
  canary capillary cautionary cherry commentary
  culinary customary dairy dictionary dietary
  dignitary disciplinary discretionary
  evolutionary extraordinary fairy February ferry
  functionary hairy hereditary honorary
  imaginary incendiary intermediary January Jerry
  legendary legionary literary luminary Mary
  mercenary military momentary monetary
  mortuary nary necessary obituary ordinary
  Perry planetary prairie proprietary pulmonary
  reactionary revolutionary sanctuary sanitary
  secretary seminary sherry solitary stationary
  temporary Terry Tipperary very visionary
  vocabulary voluntary wary

Scene (see **Seen**)

Scenery beanery greenery machinery

Scent absent accent augment cement comment
  compliment consent content dent dissent
  ferment frequent indent invent present prevent
  relent rent repent represent resent supplement
  tent torment vent

School April fool cool drool fool ghoul Liverpool
  overrule pool rule spool stool tool whirlpool

Scientific hieroglyphic horrific pacific prolific
  specific terrific

Scope (see **Hope**)

S

Score (see **Door**)

Scorn adorn airborne born Cape Horn Capricorn corn forlorn horn lovelorn Matterhorn morn mourn popcorn stillborn sworn unicorn warn worn

Scout about boy scout blow-out bout clout devout doubt eke out flout gout lout out pout roundabout route shout snout spout sprout stout tout trout wash-out worn-out

Scramble amble gamble ramble shamble

Scratch attach batch catch detach dispatch hatch latch match patch snatch

Scream beam cream deem dream esteem extreme gleam ream regime scheme seam seen steam stream supreme team teem

Screw (see **Do**)

Screwy buoy chewy dewy Drambuie gluey gooey hooey Louie phooey St. Louie

Script chipped dipped crypt equipped manuscript sipped transcript whipped zipped

Scrub Beelzebub bub club cub grub hub hubbub pub rub rub-a-dub-dub shrub snub stub sub tub

Scruple pupil

Scuba Cuba tuba

Scuffle duffle muffle ruffle shuffle truffle

S

Scum album aquarium auditorium become bum
        burdensome Christendom come cranium
        crematorium crumb curriculum drum dump
        emporium fee-fi-fo-fum glum gum gymnasium
        hum kettledrum kingdom martyrdom
        maximum meddlesome medium millennium
        minimum mum museum numb opium
        overcome pendulum petroleum platinum plum
        premium quarrelsome radium random rum
        sanitarium slum some strum succumb sum
        swum tedium thumb Tom Thumb Tweedledum
        uranium worrisome yum

Sea (see **Be**)

Seal (see **Steal**)

Search besmirch birch church lurch perch research
        search smirch

Season pleasin' reason sneezin' squeezin' teasin'
        wheezin' (see *son*)

Seat (see **Sweet**)

Secure (see **Pure**)

Seduce abuse accuse confuse cues deduce diffuse
        disuse duce excuse induce infuse introduce
        juice misuse obtuse peruse produce profuse
        reduce refuse reproduce Syracuse use

See (see **Be**)

Seed agreed breed centipede concede creed deed
        exceed feed greed heed inbreed knead lead

S

mislead need precede proceed read recede
reed secede speed stampede succeed Swede
tweed weed

Seeing agreeing being decreeing disagreeing
farseeing fleeing foreseeing freeing
guaranteeing overseeing teeing unseeing

Seek beak bleak creek eek freak leak meek reek
speak tweak weak week

Seen bean between caffeine canteen chlorine clean
codeine Colleen convene cuisine dean demean
evergreen Florentine foreseen gasoline Gene
green guillotine Halloween in-between
intervene kerosene lean lien machine marine
mean mezzanine Nazarene nectarine nicotine
obscene preen quarantine queen ravine routine
sardine scene serene spleen submarine
tambourine tangerine teen thirteen (etc.)
Vaseline velveteen wintergreen wolverine

Self elf herself himself itself myself shelf yourself

S

Sell bell belle Carmel carrousel cell clientele dell
dwell excel farewell fell gel hell hotel infidel
knell mademoiselle personnel shell smell spell
tell well yell

Selling compelling dwelling excelling expelling
foretelling fortune-telling misspelling quelling
rebelling repelling shelling smelling spelling
swelling telling underselling yelling

Semester Chester contester fester investor jester Lester molester pester protester sequester tester Westchester Winchester

Send apprehend ascend attend befriend bend blend commend comprehend condescend defend depend descend dividend end expend extend fend friend intend lend mend offend penned pretend recommend spend suspend tend transcend trend unbend

Sensational congregational creational educational inspirational recreational representational

Sense (see **Fence**)

Sensed against condensed fenced

Senses commences defenses dispenses fences offenses tenses

Sensing condensing dispensing fencing incensing recompensing

Sent (see **Bent**)

Sentence repentance

Sequel equal

Serenity amenity obscenity

Serial cereal immaterial material managerial ministerial

Serious (see **Us**)

Sermon determine German merman vermin

S

Serve conserve curve deserve nerve observe preserve reserve swerve

Settle kettle metal mettle petal resettle settle

Severe (see **Near**)

Sewer bluer brewer doer fewer interviewer newer pursuer reviewer skewer truer viewer wooer

Sex complex decks duplex ex flex necks pecks reflex Rolidex specs Tex unisex

Shack (see **Sack**)

Shackle cackle crackle hackle ramshackle tackle

Shade (see **Afraid**)

Shake ache bake brake break cake fake flake forsake headache heartache keepsake make mistake opaque quake rake sake snake stake steak take wake

Shall canal chorale gal morale pal

Shallow callow fallow hallow mallow marshmallow tallow

Sham (see **Am**)

Shamble amble gamble ramble scramble

Shame acclaim aim became blame came claim exclaim fame flame frame game inflame lame maim name proclaim same tame

Shanty aunty panty scanty

Shape (see **Ape**)

S

Shark   aardvark arc ark bark dark embark hark lark
        mark narc park patriarch remark spark stark

Sharp   carp harp

She   (see **Be**)

Shelf   elf herself himself itself myself self yourself

Shelter   belter smelter swelter

Shelve   delve twelve

Shepherd   leopard peppered

Shield   battlefield Chesterfield field wield yield

Shift   drift gift lift spendthrift swift thrift

Shifty   fifty nifty thrifty

Shine   align asinine assign benign combine
        concubine confine consign decline define
        design dine divine entwine fine incline line
        malign mine nine outshine pine porcupine
        recline refine resign Rhine shrine sign spine
        stein swine twine underline undermine vine
        whine wine

Ship   (see **Trip**)

Shirt   alert avert blurt concert convert curt desert
        dessert dirt divert exert expert extrovert flirt
        hurt insert introvert invert pervert skirt squirt
        subvert yogurt

Shock   Bangkok beanstalk boondock clock cock
        cornstalk crock deadlock defrock dock flintlock
        flock frock gawk gridlock hawk hock J.S. Bach

jock knock Little Rock livestock lock mock
Mohawk padlock peacock rock sidewalk small
talk smock sock squawk stalk stock talk
tomahawk unlock walk wok

Shoe (see **Do**)

Shoot absolute acute astute attribute beaut boot
brute Butte chute commute compute
constitute coot cute destitute dilute dispute
disrepute dissolute electrocute enroute
execute flute fruit hoot loot lute minute moot
mute newt parachute persecute pollute
prosecute prostitute pursuit recruit refute
repute resolute root route scoot snoot
substitute suit toot transmute uproot

Shop (see **Drop**)

Short abort assort cavort comfort contort court
davenport deport distort escort exhort export
extort fort import passport port quart report
resort retort short snort sort sport support
thwart tort transport wart

S

Shot apricot blot Camelot clot cot cybot dot forget-
me-not forgot fought gavotte got hot hot-shot
jot knot lot not plot pot robot rot slingshot
somewhat spot squat swat tot trot watt what
yacht

Should brotherhood could fatherhood firewood
good Hollywood hood likelihood livelihood

misunderstood motherhood neighborhood
sisterhood stood understood withstood
womanhood wood would

Shout about boy scout blow-out bout clout devout
doubt eke out flout gout lout pout roundabout
route scout snout spout sprout stout tout trout
wash-out worn-out

Shove above dove glove ladylove love mourning
dove of turtle dove

Shower cauliflower cower deflower empower flower
horsepower plower power tower (see *our*)

Shown (see **Stone**)

Shrank bank blank clank crank dank drank flank
frank hank outrank plank prank rank sank spank
stank tank thank yank

Shrewd brood clued conclude crude dude exclude
food glued include intrude misconstrued mood
preclude prude rude seclude wooed

Shrewdly crudely lewdly rudely

Shrimp blimp gimp limp pimp skimp wimp

Shrine (see **Fine**)

Shrink blink brink chink clink drink fink ink kink link
mink pink rink sink slink stink wink zinc

Shroud allowed aloud cloud crowd enshroud loud
plowed proud thundercloud

Shuffle duffle muffle ruffle truffle

Shut but butt cut glut gut halibut hut King Tut mutt
       nut putt rut scuttlebutt slut smut strut uncut

Shy (see **Cry**)

Shyly dryly highly Reilly slyly spryly wily wryly

Sick arithmetic arsenic brick candlestick candlewick
       Catholic chick click flick heartsick hick kick lick
       limerick love-sick lunatic maverick nick pick
       slick stick thick tic tick wick

Side beside bonafide bride collide confide
       countryside decide defied died dignified divide
       eyed fireside guide hide hillside homicide
       inside lied outside override pride provide
       reside ride slide snide stride subdivide subside
       suicide tide tried wide yuletide

Sight appetite bite blight bright byte contrite
        copyright daylight delight despite dynamite
        excite Fahrenheit fight flight fright headlight
        height ignite invite kite knight light midnight
        might moonlight night outright parasite plight
        polite quite recite reunite right satellite site
        sleight slight spite starlight sunlight tight trite
        twilight unite white write

Sign align asinine assign benign combine concubine
       confine consign decline define design dine
       divine entwine fine incline line malign mine
       nine outshine pine porcupine recline refine
       resign Rhine shine shrine spine stein swine
       twine underline undermine vine whine wine

S

Signature (see **Pure**)

Signify dignify (see *cry*)

Silk bilk ilk milk

Silly Billy Chile Chili chilly dilly filly frilly hillbilly
hilly lily Philly Piccadilly piccalilli shrilly willy-
nilly

Simmer dimmer glimmer grimmer primmer skimmer
slimmer swimmer trimmer

Simple dimple pimple

Sin aspirin been begin Berlin bin chagrin chin
discipline feminine fin genuine gin grin
harlequin heroine in inn kin mandolin
mannequin masculine moccasin origin pin
saccharine shin skin spin thick-and-thin thin
tin twin violin within win

Since convince hints mints prince rinse wince

Sincere (see **Near**)

Sincerity austerity dexterity insincerity posterity
prosperity severity

Sing anything bring cling ding evening everything
fling king ring sling spring sting string swing
thing wing wring (add "ing" to "action" words,
i.e., run(ning), etc.)

Single intermingle jingle Kris Kringle mingle shingle
tingle

Sink blink brink chink clink drink fink ink kink link

mink pink rink shrink slink stink think wink zinc

Sinner B.F. Skinner beginner breadwinner dinner inner skinner spinner thinner winner

Sinister administer minister

Siphon hyphen

Sir (see **Her**)

Sirloin purloin

Sister assister blister magister mister resister twister (see *her*)

Sit befit bit fit 'git grit kit knit hit it lit mitt nit-wit pit quit twit unfit ultimate wit zit

Size (see **Lies**)

Sizzle chisel drizzle fizzle frizzle grizzle swizzle

Skate (see **Ate**)

Skeptic antiseptic septic

Sketch catch etch fetch kvetch retch stretch wretch

Skid bid did forbid grid hid invalid lid Madrid pyramid rid slid squid

Skin (see **Been**)

Skinny New Guinea ninny tinny

Skirt (see **Shirt**)

Skull annul cull dull gull hull lull mull scull

Skunk bunk chunk clunk cyberpunk drunk dunk flunk funk hunk junk monk plunk punk shrunk slunk spunk stunk sunk trunk

S

Sky (see **Cry**)

Skyscraper caper draper escaper paper raper
    scraper shaper taper

Slacker attacker backer blacker cracker hacker
    hijacker nutcracker packer ransacker smacker
    tracker

Slam (see **Am**)

Slang bang boomerang clang dang fang orangutan
    rang sang sprang

Slant (see **Ant**)

Slap cap chap clap flap gap handicap lap map
    mishap nap rap sap scrap snap strap tap trap
    wrap zap

Slaughter blotter daughter hotter otter plotter
    spotter squatter trotter water

Slave behave brave cave concave crave engrave
    forgave gave grave knave pave rave save shave
    waive wave

Slavery (see **Be**)

Sleaze (see **Ease**)

Sled (see **Said**)

Sleep barkeep cheep creep deep heap keep leap
    peep reap seep sheep steep sweep weep

Sleeve achieve believe bereave conceive disbelieve
    eve grieve heave leave perceive receive relieve
    reprieve retrieve weave

S

Sleigh (see **Say**)

Slept accept adept crept except intercept kept
    overslept stepped swept wept

Sleuth booth couth Duluth tooth truth uncouth
    youth

Slid bid did forbid grid hid invalid lid Madrid
    pyramid rid skid squid

Slim brim dim grim gym hymn limb pseudonym
    skim swim trim whim

Slime chime climb crime dime I'm lime mime
    pantomime prime rhyme summertime thyme
    time

Slob blob bob cob fob gob hob hobnob job knob lob
    mob nob rob snob sob swab throb

Sloppy choppy copy floppy hoppy poppy soppy

Slow (see **Blow**)

Slum (see **Scum**)

Slumber cucumber cumber encumber lumber
    number umber

Slut (see **But**)

Small all ball bawl brawl call crawl doll drawl fall gall
    haul install mall maul Montreal nightfall
    overhaul parasol pitfall protocol rainfall scrawl
    shawl snowfall sprawl stall tall thrall wall
    waterfall y'all

Smart apart art cart chart counterpart dart depart
    heart mart part start sweetheart tart upstart

Prefixes: pre, re, in, con, de, mis

Smash ash balderdash bash brash cash clash crash dash flash gnash rash rehash slash splash stash thrash trash

Smell bell belle Carmel carrousel cell clientele dell dwell excel farewell fell gel hell hotel infidel knell mademoiselle personnel sell shell spell tell well yell

Smile aisle awhile beguile bile compile crocodile defile file isle juvenile meanwhile mile Nile pile rile style tile vile while wile worthwhile

Smiling beguiling compiling defiling filing piling reconciling reviling styling tiling

Smirk clerk handiwork irk jerk Kirk lurk murk overwork perk quirk shirk Turk work

Smoke (see **Joke**)

Smooch hooch mooch pooch

Smooth soothe

Smudge budge drudge fudge grudge judge misjudge nudge

Smug bug drug dug jug hug lug mug plug pug rug shrug slug snug thug tug

Smuggle juggle snuggle struggle

Smut (see **But**)

Snack (see **Sack**)

Snake ache bake brake break cake fake flake forsake headache heartache keepsake make mistake

opaque quake rake sake shake stake steak take
wake

Sniff   cliff handkerchief if stiff tiff whiff

Sniffle   piffle riffle whiffle

Snivel   civil drivel shrivel swivel

Snob   blob bob cob fob gob hob hobnob job knob
lob mob nob rob slob sob swab throb

Snow   (see **Blow**)

Snowy   blowy Bowie doughy showy

So   afro although banjo beau below bestow blow bow
buffalo bungalow calico crossbow crow depot
doe domino dough embryo escrow Eskimo flow
foe forgo fro gazebo gigolo glow go grow heigh-
ho ho-ho hobo hoe incognito indigo Joe know
long ago low Mexico mistletoe mow no oboe
oh outgrow overflow overgrow overthrow owe
Pinocchio pistachio plateau quo rainbow ratio
roe row sew slow snow Soho status quo stow
studio tally-ho though throw tiptoe to-and-fro
toe Tokyo tow tremolo undergo undertow
vertigo woe yo yo-yo

Soap   (see **Hope**)

Sob   blob bob cob fob gob hob hobnob job knob lob
mob nob rob slob snob swab throb

Sober   disrober October prober rober

Society   anxiety impropriety notoriety piety propriety
sobriety variety

S

Sock (see **Shock**)

Soda coda pagoda

Soft aloft loft oft

Sold behold blindfold bold centerfold cold fold
         foothold foretold gold hold household
         marigold mold old retold scold told uphold
         withhold

Solitaire (see **Air**)

Solitary (see **Scary**)

Solitude allude altitude aptitude attitude delude
         dude feud fortitude gratitude interlude latitude
         lewd longitude magnitude multitude nude
         prelude pursued renewed subdued sued 'tude
         you'd

Solo bolo coco gigolo piccolo polo tremolo

Solution (see **Revolution**)

Solve absolve devolve dissolve evolve involve
         revolve

Some (see **Scum**)

Some album aquarium auditorium become bum
         burdensome Christendom come cranium
         crematorium crumb curriculum drum dumb
         emporium fee-fi-fo-fum glum gum gymnasium
         hum kettledrum kingdom martyrdom
         maximum meddlesome medium millennium
         minimum mum museum numb opium

overcome pendulum petroleum platinum plum
premium quarrelsome radium random rum
sanitarium scum slum strum succumb sum
swum tedium thumb Tom Thumb Tweedledum
uranium worrisome yum

Somebody body embody gaudy lawdy nobody
shoddy toddy

Son anyone begun bun comparison done everyone
fun Galveston gun hon Hun jettison none nun
oblivion one outdone outrun overdone overrun
phenomenon pun run shun simpleton skeleton
stun sun ton unison venison won

Song along belong bong ding-dong gong Hong Kong
long Ping-Pong prong strong throng wrong

Soon afternoon baboon balloon bassoon boon
buffoon cartoon cocoon coon croon goon
harpoon harvest moon honeymoon lagoon
lampoon loon maroon monsoon moon noon
platoon prune raccoon saloon Saskatoon
spittoon swoon tycoon typhoon (see *tune*)

Soothe smooth

Sorrow borrow morrow sorrow tomorrow

Sought (see **Thought**)

Sound abound around astound background
battleground bloodhound bound compound
confound downed dumbfound found ground
hound impound merry-go-round mound pound

S

profound renowned resound round spellbound surround underground wound

Soup coop droop dupe group hoop loop nincompoop poop scoop sloop stoop swoop troop troupe whoop

Source coarse course divorce endorse force horse Norse reinforce remorse resource

Space ace base bass brace case chase commonplace debase disgrace displace embrace encase erase face grace lace mace misplace pace place race replace steeplechase trace unlace vase

Spare (see **Air**)

Spark aardvark arc ark bark dark embark hark lark mark narc park patriarch remark shark stark

Sparrow arrow barrow harrow marrow narrow tarot

Sparse farce parse

Spasm bioplasm chasm enthusiasm plasm sarcasm

Spat (see **At**)

Speak beak bleak creek eek freak leak meek reek seek tweak weak week

Speech beach breach each impeach leech peach preach reach screech teach

Speed agreed breed centipede concede creed deed exceed feed greed heed inbreed knead lead mislead need precede proceed read recede reed secede seed stampede succeed Swede tweed weed

Spent (see **Bent**)

Sperm affirm confirm firm germ reaffirm squirm term worm

Spider chider cider decider divider glider insider low-rider outsider provider rider slider wider

Splash ash balderdash bash brash cash clash crash dash flash gnash rash rehash slash smash stash thrash trash

Splendor (see **Tender**)

Spoil broil coil foil loyal oil recoil royal toil turmoil

Spoken broken heartbroken Hoboken jokin' oaken outspoken smokin' soakin' token

Sponge lunge plunge

Spook fluke kook

Spooky fluky kooky pooky

Sport (see **Short**)

Spot (see **Pot**)

Spouse blouse douse grouse house louse madhouse mouse outhouse penthouse slaughterhouse souse

Sprang bang boomerang clang dang fang orangutan rang sang slang

Sprinkle crinkle periwinkle tinkle twinkle wrinkle

Spurn (see **Learn**)

Squabble bobble cobble gobble hobble wobble

Squalor bawler brawler call 'er caller choler collar crawler dollar hauler mauler scrawler smaller taller

Squander condor conned 'er fonder launder ponder wander yonder

Square (see **Air**)

Squeeze (see **Ease**)

Squish devilish dish fish gibberish impoverish swish wish

Stab blab cab crab dab drab gab grab jab lab nab scab tab

Stack (see **Sack**)

Staff calf carafe epitaph giraffe graph laugh paragraph phonograph photograph polygraph riffraff telegraph

Stage age cage gage page rampage sage wage

Stagger bagger bragger carpet-bagger dagger swagger tagger

Stale (see **Ale**)

Stall all ball bawl brawl call crawl doll drawl fall gall haul install mall maul Montreal nightfall overhaul parasol pitfall protocol rainfall scrawl shawl small snowfall sprawl tall thrall wall waterfall y'all

S

Stallion battalion Italian medallion rapscallion scallion

Stamp amp camp champ clamp cramp damp lamp ramp vamp

Stand and band brand canned command contraband demand expand fanned grand hand land panned planned reprimand Rio Grande sand

Stank bank blank clank crank dank drank flank frank hank outrank plank prank rank sank shrank spank tank thank yank

Stanza bonanza extravaganza

Staple maple papal

Star are bar bazaar bizarre car caviar cigar czar disbar far guitar jar par scar spar tar

Starch arch march parch

Stare (see **Air**)

Start apart art cart chart counterpart dart depart heart mart part smart sweetheart tart upstart

Starve carve

Static (see **Attic**)

Stay (see **Say**)

Steal appeal automobile Bastille Camille conceal deal eel feel genteel he'll heal heel ideal kneel meal mobile peel real reel repeal reveal seal she'll spiel squeal steel veal we'll wheel zeal

S

Steel (see **Steal**)

Stem Bethlehem condemn gem hem phlegm
requiem them

Step footstep pep rep

Stew (see **Do**)

Stick (see **Pick**)

Still bill chill daffodil distill drill fill frill fulfill gill
grill hill ill imbecile instill kill mill nil quill
shrill sill skill spill swill thrill till trill until
whippoorwill will windmill windowsill

Stink blink brink chink clink drink fink ink kink link
mink pink rink shrink sink slink wink zinc

Stir (see **Her**)

Stirrup chirrup syrup (see *up*)

Stolen colon rollin' semicolon (see *in*)

Stomp comp pomp romp swamp tromp

Stone alone atone backbone baritone blown bone
chaperone clone condone cone cornerstone
cyclone Dictaphone flown full-blown full-grown
gramophone grindstone groan grown
headstone known loan lone microphone
milestone moan monotone mown overgrown
overthrown own phone postpone prone
saxophone sewn shown telephone thrown tone
trombone unknown xylophone zone

Stood brotherhood could fatherhood firewood good

Hollywood hood likelihood livelihood
misunderstood motherhood neighborhood
should sisterhood understood withstood
womanhood wood would

Stop chop cop crop drop eavesdrop flop hop
lollipop mop plop pop prop raindrop shop
swap tip-top whop

Store (see **Door**)

Stork cork fork New York pitchfork pork torque
uncork

Storm chloroform conform deform form inform norm
perform rainstorm reform snowstorm swarm
transform uniform warm

Story accusatory allegory category dormitory dory
glory gory hunky-dory laboratory Lori
obligatory observatory oratory Peter Lorre
quarry reformatory retaliatory sorry story
territory Tory

Strange arrange change derange estrange exchange
range

Strangle angle dangle entangle jangle mangle
spangle tangle triangle wrangle

Stream beam cream deem dream esteem extreme
gleam ream regime scheme scream seam seen
steam supreme team teem

Street (see **Sweet**)

Strength length

Stress (see **Confess**)

Stricken chicken quicken sicken thicken (see *in*)

Strict addict conflict constrict contradict convict
   derelict evict flicked inflict licked predict
   pricked

Strike bike hike like mike spike tyke

Strong along belong bong ding-dong gong Hong
   Kong long Ping-Pong prong song throng wrong

Stronger longer

Struck amuck buck chuck cluck deduct duck horror-
   struck luck muck pluck potluck puck suck truck
   tuck

Struggle juggle smuggle snuggle

Strum (see **Scum**)

Strung (see **Young**)

Strut (see **But**)

S

Stud blood bud cud dud flood mud scud spud thud

Stuff (see **Bluff**)

Stuffy fluffy huffy puffy

Stump bump chump clump dump hump jump lump
   plump rump slump thump trump ump

Stunk bunk chunk clunk cyberpunk drunk dunk flunk
   funk hunk junk monk plunk punk shrunk skunk
   slunk spunk sunk trunk

Stunt affront blunt brunt bunt confront forefront front grunt hunt punt runt shunt

Stupid Cupid

Style (see **Smile**)

Subject (see **Defect**)

Subtle cuttle rebuttal scuttle shuttle (see *puddle*)

Suburb blurb 'burb curb disturb herb perturb Serb superb verb

Such clutch crutch Dutch hutch inasmuch much retouch touch

Suck amuck buck chuck cluck deduct duck horror-struck luck muck pluck potluck puck struck truck tuck

Sue (see **Knew**)

Suffer bluffer buffer duffer gruffer puffer rougher tougher

Suggestion congestion digestion indigestion ingestion question

Suicidal bridal bridle homicidal idle idol tidal

Suit (see **Shoot**)

Suite (see **Sweet**)

Suitor commuter computer cuter muter neuter persecutor polluter prosecutor tutor

Sulk bulk hulk

Summer comer drummer dumber hummer newcomer strummer

S

Sun　(see **Son**)

Sung　among clung dung flung high-strung hung lung rung slung sprung strung stung swung tongue unstrung unsung wrung young

Sunk　bunk chunk clunk cyberpunk drunk dunk flunk funk hunk junk monk plunk punk shrunk skunk slunk spunk stunk trunk

Sunny　bunny funny honey money

Sunrise　(see **Lies**)

Sunset　alphabet bayonet bet brunette cabinet cadet cigarette clarinet cornet corvette debt duet forget fret gazette get jet Joliet Juliet let luncheonette marionette met net omelet pet quartet regret roulette set silhouette Somerset sweat threat Tibet toilette upset vet 'vette violet wet yet

Super　cooper hooper looper snooper stupor trooper

Superb　blurb 'burb curb disturb herb perturb Serb suburb verb

Superficial　artificial beneficial initial judicial official sacrificial

Superior　exterior inferior interior ulterior

Superstition　(see **Tradition**)

Supper　upper

Supportive　(See **Abortive**)

Sure　allure armature assure brochure caricature

cocksure cure demure endure ensure
expenditure immature impure insecure insure
liqueur literature lure manicure manure mature
miniature obscure overture pedicure premature
pure reassure secure signature tablature
temperature your

Surf nerf serf turf

Surge (see **Verge**)

Surgeon burgeon emergin' mergin' sturgeon surgin'
     urgin' virgin

Surgery perjury

Survival arrival revival rival

Suspect (see **Defect**)

Suspected affected bisected corrected defected
     deflected detected directed disaffected
     dissected effected erected expected infected
     inflected inspected intersected neglected
     objected perfected protected reflected
     respected resurrected unaffected unexpected

Suspicious (see **Vicious**)

Swagger carpetbagger dagger stagger

Swallow Apollo follow hollow wallow

Swam (see **Am**)

Swamp prompt stomp

Swan Amazon Babylon begone bonbon Bonn brawn
     chiffon con Don dawn drawn fawn gone

hexagon John lawn lexicon octagon on Oregon pawn pentagon silicon undergone upon withdrawn wanton yawn

Swear affair air anywhere aware bare bear billionaire blare care chair compare dare debonair declare despair disrepair elsewhere everywhere fair fare flair glare hair hare heir impair legionnaire mare midair millionaire nightmare pair pare pear Pierre prayer prepare rare ready-to-wear repair scare snare solitaire somewhere spare square stair stare tear their there thoroughfare unaware underwear unfair ware wear where

Sweat (see **Sunset**)

Sweater better debtor getter letter setter wetter

Sweet athlete beat beet bittersweet bleat cheat compete complete conceit concrete deceit defeat delete deplete discreet discrete eat elite feat feet fleet greet heat incomplete indiscreet meat meet mistreat neat obsolete parakeet receipt repeat retreat seat sheet sleet street suite treat wheat

Sweetly completely concretely discreetly indiscreetly fleetly neatly

Sweety meaty treaty

Swept accept adept crept except intercept kept overslept slept stepped wept

Swift drift gift lift shift spendthrift thrift

S

Swig big dig fig gig jig pig rig thingamajig twig wig

Swim brim dim grim gym hymn limb pseudonym
skim slim trim whim

Swindle dwindle kindle rekindle spindle

Swing (see **Sing**)

Swipe archetype gripe hype pipe prototype ripe
stereotype stripe type wipe

Swirl curl earl girl hurl pearl twirl whirl

Switch bewitch bitch ditch enrich glitch hitch pitch
rich snitch stitch twitch which

Swollen bowlin' rollin' stolen

Swamp comp pomp romp stomp tromp

Sword aboard accord afford award board bored ford
harpsichord hoard lord overboard poured
reward shuffleboard soared ward

Swore (see **Door**)

Syllable fillable tillable

Symbol cymbal nimble thimble

S

swipe
ripe

s w i m
swirl
pearl
whim

T

Tab blab cab crab dab drab gab grab jab lab nab scab slab stab

Table (see **Able**)

Tackle cackle crackle hackle ramshackle shackle

Tad (see **Mad**)

Tag bag brag drag flag gag hag lag mag nag rag sag shag slag snag stag swag wag

Take ache bake brake break cake fake flake forsake headache heartache keepsake make mistake opaque quake rake shake snake stake steak wake

Taken achin' bacon fakin' forsaken Jamaican makin' mistaken overtaken shaken undertaken unshaken waken

Talk Bangkok beanstalk boondock cock cornstalk clock crock deadlock defrock dock flintlock flock frock gawk gridlock hawk hock J.S. Bach jock knock Little Rock livestock lock mock Mohawk padlock peacock rock shock sidewalk small smock sock squawk stalk stock tomahawk unlock walk wok

Tall all ball bawl brawl call crawl doll drawl fall gall haul install mall maul Montreal nightfall overhaul parasol pitfall protocol rainfall scrawl shawl small snowfall sprawl stall thrall wall

T

waterfall y'all

Tame (see **Aim**)

Tangle angle dangle entangle jangle mangle spangle
strangle triangle wrangle

Tango fandango mango

Tank bank blank clank crank dank drank flank frank
hank outrank plank prank rank sank shrank
spank stank thank yank

Tap cap chap clap flap gap handicap lap map
mishap nap rap sap scrap slap snap strap trap
wrap zap

Tape (see **Ape**)

Tarnish garnish varnish

Tarot arrow barrow harrow marrow narrow sparrow

Task ask bask cask flask mask masque

Taste baste aftertaste braced chaste distaste faced
freckle-faced haste hatchet-faced lambaste
paste waist waste

Tattoo (see **Do**)

Tavern cavern

Tax ax backs fax jacks lax max relax packs Saks sax
slacks wax

Taxes axes battle-axes relaxes saxes waxes

Tea (see **Be**)

Teach beach breach each impeach leech peach
preach reach screech speech

Teacher bleacher creature feature preacher screecher

Team beam cream deem dream esteem extreme gleam ream regime scheme scream seam seen steam stream supreme teem

Tear adhere appear atmosphere auctioneer beer bombardier career cashier cavalier chandelier cheer clear dear deer disappear ear engineer fear financier frontier gear hear hemisphere here insincere interfere jeer lavaliere leer mere mountaineer near overhear overseer peer persevere pioneer queer racketeer reappear rear revere seer severe shear sheer sincere smear sneer spear sphere stratosphere veneer volunteer year

Tearful cheerful earful fearful

Tease (see **Ease**)

Tedium medium (see *some*)

Teeny Bellini fettucini genie meany Mussolini scaloppini weenie

Teeth beneath heath teeth underneath wreath

Telegram (see **Am**)

Television (see **Vision**)

Tell bell belle Carmel carrousel cell clientele dell dwell excel farewell fell gel hell hotel infidel knell mademoiselle personnel sell shell smell spell well yell

T

Temperature (see **Pure**)

Tempt attempt contempt dreamt exempt unkempt

Tempted attempted exempted pre-empted

Tender bender blender contender defender extender
fender gender lender mender offender
pretender sender slender spender splendor
surrender suspender vendor weekender

Tennis menace

Tense (see **Fence**)

Tension abstention apprehension ascension
attention comprehension condescension
convention dissension detention dimension
dissension extension intention intervention
invention mention retention suspension

Term affirm confirm firm germ reaffirm sperm
squirm worm

Terrific hieroglyphic horrific pacific prolific scientific
specific

Terror bearer carer darer error wearer

Testimony acrimony alimony baloney bony crony
macaroni matrimony patrimony phony pony
sanctimony stony Tony

Text context flexed next pretext

Thank bank blank clank crank dank drank flank frank
hank outrank plank prank rank sank shrank
spank stank tank yank

Thankful   tankful (see *bull*)

Thaw   (see **Draw**)

Theft   deft left

Them   Bethlehem condemn gem hem phlegm requiem stem

Then   amen citizen den fen hen hydrogen Ken oxygen pen regimen specimen ten yen zen

Theory   teary weary (see *be*)

There   affair air anywhere aware bare bear billionaire blare care chair compare dare debonair declare despair disrepair elsewhere everywhere fair fare flair glare hair hare heir impair legionnaire mare midair millionaire nightmare pair pare pear Pierre prayer prepare rare ready-to-wear repair scare snare solitaire somewhere spare square stair stare swear tear their thoroughfare unaware underwear unfair ware wear where

Thick   arithmetic arsenic brick candlestick candlewick Catholic chick click flick heartsick hick kick lick limerick love-sick lunatic maverick nick pick sick slick stick tic tick wick

Thief   beef belief brief chief disbelief grief leaf relief

Thin   (see **Been**)

Thing   (see **Sing**)

Think   blink brink chink clink drink fink ink kink link mink pink rink shrink sink slink stink wink zinc

Thirst   burst cursed first nursed outburst versed

worst

This abyss amiss analysis armistice bliss carcass
cowardice dismiss emphasis hiss hypothesis
kiss miss nemesis prejudice Swiss synthesis

Thorough borough burrow furrow

Thought astronaut bought brought caught
cosmonaut fought naught ought overwrought
sought taught wrought

Threat (see **Sunset**)

Thrill bill chill daffodil distill drill fill frill fulfill gill
grill hill ill imbecile instill kill mill nil quill
shrill sill skill spill still swill till trill until
whippoorwill will windmill windowsill

Thriller caterpillar chiller distiller driller filler
instiller killer pillar shriller spiller swiller tiller

Throat afloat antidote bloat boat coat connote
denote dote float footnote gloat goat misquote
moat note oat overcoat promote quote remote
riverboat rote smote tote underwrote vote
wrote

Throb blob bob cob gob hob hobnob job knob lob
mob nob rob slob snob sob

Throw (see **Blow**)

Thrown alone atone backbone baritone blown bone
chaperone clone condone cone cornerstone
cyclone Dictaphone flown full-blown full-grown
gramophone grindstone groan grown

T

headstone known loan lone microphone milestone moan monotone mown overgrown overthrown own phone postpone prone saxophone sewn shown stone telephone tone trombone unknown xylophone zone

Thrust (see **Trust**)

Thumb album aquarium auditorium become bum burdensome Christendom come cranium crematorium crumb curriculum dumb drum emporium fee-fi-fo-fum glum gum gymnasium hum kettledrum kingdom martyrdom maximum meddlesome medium millennium minimum mum museum numb opium overcome pendulum petroleum platinum plum premium quarrelsome radium random rum sanitarium scum slum some strum succumb sum swum tedium Tom Thumb Tweedledum uranium worrisome yum

Thunder blunder plunder under wonder

Thus (see **Us**)

Tick arithmetic arsenic brick candlestick candlewick Catholic chick click flick heartsick hick kick lick limerick love-sick lunatic maverick nick pick sick slick stick thick tic wick

Ticket cricket picket thicket wicket (see **it**)

Ticking bricking clicking flicking kicking licking pricking slicking sticking

Tide beside bonafide bride collide confide

countryside decide defied died dignified divide
eyed fireside guide hide hillside homicide
inside lied outside override pride provide
reside ride side slide snide stride subdivide
subside suicide tried wide yuletide

Tight (see **Write**)

Tilt built guilt hilt jilt kilt quilt spilt stilt Vanderbilt
wilt

Time chime climb crime dime I'm lime mime
pantomime prime rhyme slime summertime
thyme

Tingle intermingle jingle Kris Kringle mingle shingle
single

Tint flint hint lint mint peppermint print spearmint
splint sprint squint

Tip battleship chip clip dip drip equip flip grip gyp
hip lip nip quip rip scrip ship slip snip strip trip
whip zip

Tipsy dipsy gypsy Poughkeepsie

Tire (see **Fire**)

Tissue issue (see *you*)

Titanic (see **Volcanic**)

Title entitle recital vital

Tizzy busy dizzy frizzy Lizzie tin lizzie

To (see **Do**)

Toad (see **Road**)

T

Toast boast coast foremost furthermost ghost host innermost most post roast whipping post

Toga Saratoga yoga

Together altogether feather Heather leather tether weather whether (see her)

Toggle boggle boondoggle goggle

Toil broil coil foil loyal oil recoil royal spoil turmoil

Told behold blindfold bold centerfold cold fold foothold foretold gold hold household marigold mold old retold scold sold uphold withhold

Toll (see **Roll**)

Tomorrow borrow morrow sorrow

Ton anyone begun bun comparison done everyone fun Galveston gun hon Hun jettison none nun oblivion one outdone outrun overdone overrun phenomenon pun run shun simpleton skeleton son stun sun ton unison venison won

Tongue (see **Young**)

Tonic catatonic chronic diatonic enharmonic harmonic ironic monophonic philharmonic phonic platonic polyphonic sonic symphonic

Took book brook cook crook hook look mistook nook outlook rook shook undertook

Tool April fool cool drool fool ghoul Liverpool overrule pool rule school spool stool whirlpool

Tooth booth couth Duluth sleuth truth uncouth
      youth

Torch porch scorch

Tornado bravado Colorado desperado El Dorado
      Laredo Mikado

Toss across albatross boss cross double-cross floss
      gloss loss moss rhinoceros sauce

Total anecdotal antidotal

Touch clutch crutch Dutch hutch inasmuch much
      retouch such

Touches clutches crutches

Tough bluff buff cuff duff enough fluff gruff huff muff
      powder puff rough scruff scuff snuff stuff

Towel bowel dowel trowel vowel

Tower cauliflower cower deflower empower flower
      horsepower plower power shower (see *our*, *her*)

Town brown clown crown down downtown drown
      frown gown hand-me-down noun renown
      tumble-down upside down uptown

Toy ahoy annoy boy buoy convoy corduroy coy decoy
      destroy employ enjoy Illinois joy ploy Roy
      Savoy soy troy viceroy

Trace (see **Space**)

Tracer ace 'er eraser face 'er pacer place 'er (see *her*)

Track almanac attack back black bric-a-brac Cadillac
      cardiac clickety-clack egomaniac feedback hack

Hackensack haystack jack kleptomaniac knack lack maniac pack plaque Pontiac prozac quack rack sack shack slack snack stack tack whack yak zodiac

Traction (see **Action**)

Trade (see **Afraid**)

Tradition acquisition addition admission ambition ammunition attrition audition coalition commission competition composition condition definition demolition deposition disposition edition electrician emission exhibition expedition exposition extradition fission ignition imposition inhibition inquisition intermission intuition magician mathematician mission musician nutrition omission opposition partition permission petition physician politician position prohibition proposition recognition rendition repetition requisition statistician submission superstition technician transmission transposition transition tuition (see *in*)

Tragic magic

Trailer inhaler jailer sailor staler wailer whaler

Train abstain again airplane arraign ascertain attain brain Cain campaign cane chain champagne cocaine complain contain crane detain disdain domain drain entertain explain feign gain grain humane hurricane hydroplane insane lane

main Maine maintain mane migraine obtain
ordain pain pane pertain plain plane profane
propane rain refrain reign rein remain sane
slain Spain sprain stain strain sustain vain
vane vein wane windowpane

Trait (see **Ate**)

Trance advance ants chance circumstance dance
enhance extravagance finance France glance
lance pants prance romance stance

Transplant (see **Ant**)

Trap cap chap clap flap gap handicap lap map
mishap nap rap sap scrap slap snap strap tap
wrap zap

Trapeze (see **Ease**)

Trash ash balderdash bash brash cash clash crash
dash flash gnash rash rehash slash smash
splash stash thrash

Traumatic (see **Attic**)

Travel gavel gravel ravel unravel

Treasure displeasure measure pleasure

Treat (see **Sweet**)

Tree (see **Be**)

Tremendous horrendous stupendous (see *us*)

Trench bench clench drench French monkey wrench
quench stench wench wrench

Trend (see **Friend**)

Trial denial dial retrial self-denial viol

Triangle angle dangle entangle jangle mangle spangle strangle tangle wrangle

Tribe bribe circumscribe describe jibe prescribe scribe subscribe

Trigger bigger chigger digger rigger rigor swigger tigger vigor

Trio Cleo Leo Rio

Trip battleship chip clip dip drip equip flip grip gyp hip lip nip quip rip scrip ship slip snip strip tip whip zip

Trooper cooper hooper looper snooper stupor super

Trot (see Pot)

Troubadour (see **Door**)

Trouble bubble double rubble stubble

Troublemaker (see **Acre**)

Truce caboose goose loose moose noose papoose recluse spruce vamoose

Truck amuck buck chuck cluck deduct duck horror-struck luck muck pluck potluck puck struck suck tuck

Trucker bucker chucker clucker pucker sapsucker seersucker sucker (see *her*)

True (see **Do**)

Truest bluest newest

Truly coolie coolly duly newly ruly unduly unruly

Trumpet bump it crumpet dump it lump it strumpet
    thump it

Trunk bunk chunk clunk cyberpunk drunk dunk flunk
    funk hunk junk monk plunk punk shrunk skunk
    slunk spunk stunk sunk

Trust adjust August bust crust disgust distrust
    encrust entrust gust just lust mistrust must
    robust rust thrust unjust

Truth booth couth Duluth sleuth tooth uncouth
    youth

Try alibi amplify banzai barfly butterfly buy by bye
    certify clarify crucify cry defy deify deny die
    dignify diversify dragonfly drive-by dry dye eye
    firefly fly fry glorify gratify guy high horrify I
    identify imply July justify lie lullaby modify my
    mystify notify passerby pie pry qualify rely rye
    satisfy sci-fi shy sigh signify simplify sky sly
    specify spry spy terrify testify thigh tie underlie
    verify why

Tub Beelzebub bub club cub grub hub hubbub pub
    rub rub-a-dub-dub scrub shrub snub stub sub

Tube boob cube rube

Tug bug drug dug jug hug lug mug plug pug rug
    shrug slug smug snug thug

Tuition (see **Tradition**)

Tulip julep

Tumor bloomer boomer consumer humor rumor

Tune attune commune dune immune impugn inopportune June (see *moon*)

Tunnel funnel

Turf nerf serf surf

Turkey Albuquerque murky perky quirky

Turmoil broil coil foil loyal oil recoil royal spoil toil

Turn adjourn burn churn concern discern earn fern intern kern learn overturn return sojourn spurn stern taciturn urn yearn

Turtle fertile girdle myrtle

Tusk dusk husk musk

Twice advice concise device dice entice ice lice mice nice paradise precise price rice sacrifice spice splice suffice thrice vice

Twilight highlight skylight (see *light*)

Twin (see **Been**)

Twinkle crinkle periwinkle sprinkle tinkle wrinkle

Twirp blurp burp chirp usurp Wyatt Earp

Twist (see **Mist**)

Twisted assisted cysted enlisted existed fisted insisted listed misted persisted resisted subsisted

Twister assister blister magister mister resister sister (see *her*)

Type archetype gripe hype pipe prototype ripe stereotype stripe swipe wipe

Tyrant aspirant

U

Udder rudder shudder

Ugly smugly snugly

Ulcer (see **Her**)

Ultimate befit bit fit 'git grit kit knit hit it lit mitt nit-wit pit quit sit twit unfit wit zit

Umbrella Béla fella' Stella

Ump bump chump clump dump hump jump lump plump rump slump stump thump trump

Under blunder plunder thunder wonder

Underdog analog bog catalog clog cog dog fog demagogue dialogue epilogue flog frog grog hog jog log monologue synagogue travelogue

Undercover cover discover hover lover recover rediscover shover (see *her*)

Understood brotherhood could fatherhood firewood good Hollywood hood likelihood livelihood misunderstood motherhood neighborhood should sisterhood stood understood withstood womanhood wood would

Unicorn adorn airborne born Cape Horn Capricorn corn forlorn horn lovelorn Matterhorn morn mourn popcorn scorn seaborne stillborn sworn warn worn

Uniform chloroform conform deform form inform
norm perform rainstorm reform snowstorm
storm swarm transform warm

Union communion disunion reunion

Unite blight cite delight excite ignite incite indict
invite knight light recite requite reunite right
sight spite

Universal rehearsal reversal

Universe adverse converse curse disburse disperse
diverse hearse immerse intersperse inverse
nurse purse rehearse reverse terse transverse
traverse verse worse

Until bill chill daffodil distill drill fill frill fulfill gill
grill hill ill imbecile instill kill mill nil quill
shrill sill skill spill still swill thrill till trill
whippoorwill will windmill windowsill

Up buttercup cup fed up hard-up pick-up pup sup

Upon Amazon Babylon begone bonbon Bonn brawn
chiffon con Don dawn drawn fawn gone
hexagon John lawn lexicon octagon on Oregon
pawn pentagon silicon undergone withdrawn
wanton yawn

Uproot (see **Shoot**)

Upset alphabet bayonet bet brunette cabinet cadet
cigarette clarinet cornet corvette debt duet
forget fret gazette get jet Joliet Juliet let
luncheonette marionette met net omelet pet

quartet regret roulette set silhouette Somerset
sunset sweat threat Tibet toilette vet 'vette
violet wet yet

Urge converge dirge diverge emerge merge purge
scourge serge splurge submerge surge verge

Urgent detergent divergent emergent resurgent

Urn (see **Learn**)

Us *one syllable*
bus cuss Gus muss plus pus truss thus

two syllable
discuss

three syllable
amorous barbarous blasphemous boisterous
cancerous cankerous cavernous chivalrous
courteous curious devious dubious envious
hideous industrious infamous lecherous
ludicrous marvelous murderous nauseous
nautilus nebulous numerous octopus ominous
omnibus perilous poisonous ponderous
precarious prosperous ravenous rebellious
rigorous riotous scandalous scrupulous
sensuous curious devious dubious envious
hideous industrious infamous lecherous
ludicrous marvelous murderous nauseous
nautilus nebulous numerous octopus ominous
omnibus perilous poisonous ponderous
precarious prosperous ravenous rebellious

rigorous riotous scandalous scrupulous
sensuous serious slanderous stimulus
strenuous studious tedious tempestuous
thunderous tortuous treacherous treasonous
various villainous

four or more syllable
adventurous ambiguous androgynous
anonymous conspicuous contemptuous
continuous dangerous delirious erroneous
extraneous famous frivolous furious fuss
generous gregarious glorious gratuitous
harmonious hazardous hilarious illustrious
incredulous luxurious miscellaneous
monogamous monotonous mysterious
notorious oblivious populous posthumous
preposterous presumptuous promiscuous
simultaneous spontaneous tumultuous
uproarious victorious

Use abuse accuse confuse cues deduce diffuse
disuse duce excuse induce infuse introduce
juice misuse obtuse peruse produce profuse
reduce refuse reproduce seduce Syracuse

User abuse accuser boozer bruiser cruiser lose 'er
loser muser oozer refuse 'er refuser snoozer

Utter butter clutter cutter flutter gutter mutter putter
shutter sputter strutter stutter

U

V

Vacate (see **Ate**)

Vague plague

Vain abstain again airplane arraign ascertain attain brain Cain campaign cane chain champagne cocaine complain contain crane detain disdain domain drain entertain explain feign gain grain humane hurricane hydroplane insane lane main Maine maintain mane migraine obtain ordain pain pane pertain plain plane profane propane rain refrain reign rein remain sane slain Spain sprain stain strain sustain train vane vein wane windowpane

Valid ballad invalid salad

Valley alley dilly-dally rally Sally tally

Vamp amp camp champ clamp cramp damp lamp ramp stamp

Vandal candle dandle handle sandal scandal

Vanilla gorilla guerrilla Manila Priscilla villa

Variety anxiety impropriety notoriety piety propriety sobriety society (see **Be**)

Various (see **Us**)

Vary carry hari-kari marry miscarry parry (see *cherry*)

Vase ace base bass brace case chase commonplace

debase disgrace displace embrace encase erase face grace lace mace misplace pace place race replace space steeplechase trace unlace

Vast aghast blast cast classed contrast fast flabbergast forecast gassed last mast outlast overcast passed past

Vat (see **At**)

Vault assault cobalt exalt fault halt malt salt somersault

Vegetarian Aquarian Aryan barbarian buryin' Cesarean disciplinarian ferryin' humanitarian libertarian librarian Marion marryin' Sagittarian Unitarian veterinarian

Veil (see **Ale**)

Vendor (see **Tender**)

Vent (see **Bent**)

Venture adventure denture indenture misadventure

Verb blurb 'burb curb disturb herb perturb Serb suburb superb

Verbal gerbil herbal

Verbose adios bellicose close comatose diagnose dose engross grandiose gross morose nose overdose varicose

Verge converge dirge diverge emerge merge purge scourge serge splurge submerge surge urge

V

Vermin determine German merman sermon

Verse adverse converse curse disburse disperse
diverse hearse immerse intersperse inverse
nurse purse rehearse reverse terse transverse
traverse universe worse

Vessel nestle trestle wrestle

Veto bonito mosquito neat-o

Viaduct abduct conduct construct deduct instruct
obstruct plucked viaduct

Vice advice concise device dice entice ice lice mice
nice paradise precise price rice sacrifice spice
splice suffice thrice twice

Vicious ambitious auspicious capricious delicious
expeditious factious fictitious judicious
malicious nutritious propitious seditious
superstitious suspicious

Victory (see **Be**)

View adieu anew avenue barbecue bayou chew
choo-choo cue curfew debut dew due ensue
ewe few guru honeydew hue I.O.U. imbue
ingénue interview Jew knew lieu new Nehru
overdue pee-ewe pew preview pursue renew
residue revenue review spew subdue sue
undue yew you (see *do*)

Vigor bigger chigger digger rigger rigor swigger tigger
trigger

Vile aisle awhile beguile bile compile crocodile defile file isle juvenile meanwhile mile Nile pile rile smile style tile while wile worthwhile

Village pillage tillage

Villain billin' chillin' Dylan fillin' illin' willin' (see *in*)

Vindictive (see **Native**)

Vine (see **Fine**)

Violate (see **Ate**)

Violence (see **Fence**)

Viper bagpiper pied piper riper sniper striper swiper typer wiper

Virgin burgeon emergin' mergin' sturgeon surgeon surgin' urgin'

Virginity (see **Be**)

Visible divisible indivisible invisible

Vision collision decision derision division incision indecision precision provision revision supervision television

Vital entitle recital title

Vivid livid

Vocal focal local yokel

Vogue brogue rogue

Voice choice invoice rejoice

Void avoid alkaloid asteroid joyed Lloyd Sigmund

V

Freud tabloid toyed

Volcanic Hispanic manic mechanic monomaniac oceanic organic panic satanic titanic (see *romantic*)

Volley collie dolly finale folly golly jolly melancholy Molly Polly tamale trolley

Voodoo (see **Do**)

Vote afloat antidote bloat boat coat connote denote dote float footnote gloat goat misquote moat note oat overcoat promote quote remote riverboat rote smote throat tote underwrote wrote

Vouch couch crouch grouch ouch pouch slouch

Vow allow avow bough bow brow chow cow disavow endow frau how kowtow now ow plough plow row slough somehow sow thou wow

Vowel bowel dowel towel trowel

Vulture agriculture culture

Voice

rejoice

vogue

vogue

vulture

culture

W

Wag bag brag drag flag gag hag lag mag nag rag sag shag slag snag stag swag tag

Wage age cage gage page rampage sage stage

Waif safe

Wait (see **Ate**)

Wake ache bake brake break cake fake flake forsake headache heartache keepsake make mistake opaque quake rake shake snake stake steak take

Walk Bangkok beanstalk boondock cock cornstalk clock crock deadlock defrock dock flintlock flock frock gawk gridlock hawk hock J.S. Bach jock knock Little Rock livestock lock mock Mohawk padlock peacock rock shock sidewalk small talk smock sock squawk stalk stock talk tomahawk unlock wok

Wall all ball bawl brawl call crawl doll drawl fall gall haul install mall maul Montreal nightfall overhaul parasol pitfall protocol rainfall scrawl shawl small snowfall sprawl stall tall thrall waterfall y'all

Wallow Apollo follow hollow swallow

Wand beyond blond bond correspond fond dawned pond respond spawned vagabond yawned

Wander condor conned 'er fonder launder ponder

squander yonder

Want daunt flaunt gaunt haunt jaunt taunt

Ward (see **Lord**)

Warm chloroform conform deform form inform norm
perform rainstorm reform snowstorm storm
swarm transform uniform

Wart abort assort cavort comfort contort court
davenport deport distort escort exhort export
extort fort import passport port quart report
resort retort short snort sort sport support
thwart tort transport (see **Art**)

Wary adversary airy arbitrary beneficiary berry bury
canary capillary cautionary cherry commentary
culinary customary dairy dictionary dietary
dignitary disciplinary discretionary evolutionary
extraordinary fairy February ferry functionary
hairy hereditary honorary imaginary incendiary
intermediary January Jerry legendary legionary
literary luminary Mary mercenary military
momentary monetary mortuary nary necessary
obituary ordinary Perry planetary prairie
proprietary pulmonary reactionary
revolutionary sanctuary sanitary scary secretary
seminary sherry solitary stationary temporary
Terry Tipperary very visionary vocabulary
voluntary

Was abuzz buzz cause coz does fuzz

Was applause because cause clause claws gauze laws

W

menopause Oz pause paws Santa Claus

Wash awash frosh galosh gosh hogwash josh Macintosh posh quash slosh squash swash

Waste baste aftertaste braced chaste distaste faced freckle-faced haste hatchet-faced lambaste paste taste two-faced waist

Watch blotch botch crotch debauch hopscotch notch Scotch wristwatch

Water blotter daughter hotter otter plotter slaughter spotter squatter trotter

Wave behave brave cave concave crave engrave forgave gave grave knave pave rave save shave slave waive

Wax ax backs fax jacks lax max relax packs Saks sax slacks tax

Way array bay betray bluejay bouquet bray clay day decay delay disarray dismay display eh? essay exposé fray gay gray hay hey holiday hooray José Kay lay matinee may moiré naysay negligée obey pay play portray protégé ray résumé ricochet risqué rosé say slay sleigh soufflé stay stray sway they toupee weigh x-ray

We (see **Be**)

Wealth commonwealth health stealth

Weary bleary cheery deary dreary eerie Erie leery query teary

Weasel diesel easel measle

W

Weather altogether feather Heather leather tether
together whether (see **her**)

Weave achieve believe bereave conceive disbelieve
eve grieve heave leave perceive receive relieve
reprieve retrieve sleeve

Web deb ebb

Wed ahead bed bedspread bread bred coed dead
dread fed figurehead fled flowerbed
fountainhead gingerbread head inbred lead led
misled misread overfed read red riverbed said
shed shred sled sped spread thoroughbred
thread underfed unthread

Wedge allege dredge edge fledge hedge ledge
privilege sacrilege sledge

Weed agreed breed centipede concede creed deed
exceed feed greed heed inbreed knead lead
mislead need precede proceed read recede reed
secede seed speed stampede succeed Swede
tweed

Weep barkeep cheep creep deep heap keep leap
peep reap seep sheep sleep steep sweep

Weight (see **Ate**)

Weighty eighty Haiti matey

Weird appeared beard cleared disappeared feared
jeered neared persevered smeared speared

Welch belch squelch

Weld felled held meld upheld

W

Well bell belle Carmel carrousel cell clientele dell
dwell excel farewell fell gel hell hotel infidel
knell mademoiselle personnel sell shell smell
spell tell yell

Welt belt Celt dealt felt heartfelt melt pelt

Went (see **Bent**)

Wept accept adept crept except intercept kept
overslept slept stepped swept

Were amateur blur chauffeur concur confer
connoisseur defer demur deter fur her incur
infer inter myrrh occur per prefer purr recur sir
slur spur stir transfer voyageur whir

Wet alphabet bayonet bet brunette cabinet cadet
cigarette clarinet cornet corvette debt duet
epithet etiquette forget fret gazette get jet Joliet
Juliet let luncheonette marionette net omelet
pet quartet regret roulette set silhouette
Somerset sunset sweat threat Tibet toilette
upset vet 'vette violet yet

Wharf dwarf

What (see **But**, **Hot**)

Wheat (see **Sweet**)

Wheel appeal automobile Bastille Camille conceal
deal eel feel genteel he'll heal heel ideal kneel
meal mobile peel real reel repeal reveal seal
she'll spiel squeal steal steel veal we'll zeal

Where affair air anywhere aware bare bear billionaire

blare care chair compare dare debonair declare despair disrepair elsewhere everywhere fair fare flair glare hair hare heir impair legionnaire mare midair millionaire nightmare pair pare pear Pierre prayer prepare rare ready-to-wear repair scare snare solitaire somewhere spare square stair stare swear tear their there thoroughfare unaware underwear unfair ware wear

Which bewitch bitch ditch enrich glitch hitch pitch rich snitch stitch switch twitch

Whiff cliff handkerchief if sniff stiff tiff

While aisle awhile beguile bile compile crocodile defile file isle juvenile meanwhile mile Nile pile rile smile style tile vile wile worthwhile

Whim brim dim grim gym hymn limb pseudonym skim slim swim trim

Whimper scrimper shrimper skimper

Whip battleship chip clip dip drip equip flip grip gyp hip lip nip quip rip scrip ship slip snip strip tip trip zip

Whirl curl earl girl hurl pearl swirl twirl

Whisker brisker frisker risker

Whiskey frisky risky

Whisper crisper (see *her*)

Whistle bristle dismissal gristle missal missile sisal thistle

W

White (see **Fight**)

Whiz biz fizz friz his is quiz showbiz 'tis

Whole bowl buttonhole cajole casserole coal control
dole droll enroll goal hole loophole Maypole
mole Old King Cole oriole parole patrol pole
poll porthole role roll scroll tadpole toll troll

Whom bloom boom broom cloakroom doom entomb
flume gloom groom room tomb womb zoom

Whopper (see **Proper**)

Whore (see **Door**)

Whose blues booze bruise choose cruise lose news
ooze shoes snooze

Why alibi amplify banzai barfly butterfly buy by bye
certify clarify crucify cry defy deify deny die
dignify diversify dragonfly drive-by dry dye eye
firefly fly fry glorify gratify guy high horrify I
identify imply July justify lie lullaby modify my
mystify notify passerby pie pry qualify rely rye
satisfy sci-fi shy sigh signify simplify sky sly
specify spry spy terrify testify thigh tie try
underlie verify

Wick arithmetic arsenic brick candlestick candlewick
Catholic chick click flick heartsick hick kick lick
limerick love-sick lunatic maverick music nick
pick sick slick stick thick tic tick

Wide beside bonafide bride collide confide
countryside decide defied died dignified divide

W

eyed fireside guide hide hillside homicide
inside lied outside override pride provide reside
ride side slide snide stride subdivide subside
suicide tide tried yuletide

Wider chider cider decider divider glider insider low-
rider outsider provider rider slider spider

Wield battlefield Chesterfield field shield yield

Wife afterlife jackknife knife life strive wife

Wig big dig fig gig jig pig renege rig swig thingamajig
twig

Wiggle giggle jiggle squiggle wriggle

Wild child dialed mild piled smiled

Will bill chill daffodil distill drill frill fulfill gill grill
hill ill imbecile instill kill mill nil quill shrill sill
skill spill still swill thrill till trill until
whippoorwill will windmill windowsill

Willing billing chilling distilling drilling filling
fulfilling instilling killing milling shrilling
spilling stilling swilling thrilling tilling unwilling

Willow armadillo billow peccadillo pillow

Wilt built guilt hilt jilt kilt quilt spilt stilt tilt
Vanderbilt

Wimp blimp gimp limp pimp shrimp skimp

W

Win again aspirin been begin Berlin bin chagrin chin
discipline feminine fin genuine gin grin
harlequin heroine in inn kin mandolin
mannequin masculine moccasin origin pin

saccharine shin sin skin spin thick-and-thin thin
tin twin violin within

Wind behind bind blind find grind hind humankind
kind mastermind mind remind signed unkind
unwind wined

Wind disciplined grinned rescind sinned (see *bend*)

Wine (see **Fine**)

Wing anything bring cling ding evening everything
fling king ring sing sling spring sting string
swing thing wring (add "ing" to "action" words,
i.e., run(ning), etc.)

Wink blink brink chink clink drink fink ink kink link
mink pink rink shrink sink slink stink zinc

Winner B.F. Skinner beginner breadwinner dinner
inner sinner skinner spinner thinner

Wino albino rhino (see *know*)

Winter hinter printer splinter sprinter squinter tinter
(see *her*)

Wipe archetype gripe hype pipe prototype ripe
stereotype stripe swipe type

Wiping griping piping stereotyping striping swiping
typing

Wire acquire admire amplifier aspire attire buyer
choir conspire crier cryer desire dire drier dryer
entire esquire expire fire flier friar higher hire
inquire inspire justifier liar magnifier multiplier

mystifier perspire prior prophesier require retire satisfier sire squire supplier testifier tire transpire

Wise (see **Lies**)

Wiser advertiser adviser agonizer analyzer apologizer equalizer eulogizer exerciser fertilizer geyser harmonizer idolizer miser riser sizer surpriser

Wish devilish dish fish gibberish impoverish squish swish

Wisp crisp lisp

Wit befit bit fit 'git grit kit knit hit it lit nit-wit pit quit sit twit unfit zit

Witchcraft craft draft draught graft overdraft

Witches bitches ditches enriches hitches itches niches pitches riches stitches switches twitches

Witty city committee ditty gritty kitty pity pretty self-pity

Wizard gizzard lizard scissored

Woe (see **Blow**)

Woes arose chose close compose decompose depose disclose dispose doze enclose expose foreclose froze goes hose impose indispose interpose knows nose owes pose predispose presuppose prose recompose rose suppose those toes transpose

Woke artichoke baroque bloke broke choke cloak

coke croak evoke folk invoke joke oak poke provoke revoke smoke soak spoke stroke toke yoke

Womb bloom boom broom cloakroom doom entomb flume gloom groom room tomb whom zoom

Wonder blunder plunder under thunder

Wool bull cock-and-bull do-able full pull (see *beautiful*)

Word absurd bird blackbird bluebird curd heard herd Kurd hummingbird ladybird mockingbird overheard third yellowbird

Work clerk handiwork irk jerk Kirk lurk murk overwork perk quirk shirk smirk Turk

Worker book 'er hook 'er lurker shirker shook 'er smirker snooker took 'er (see *her*)

World underworld

Worm affirm confirm firm germ reaffirm sperm squirm term

Worn adorn airborne born Cape Horn Capricorn corn forlorn horn lovelorn Matterhorn morn mourn popcorn scorn seaborne stillborn sworn unicorn warn

Worry curry flurry fury hurry jury Missouri scurry slurry surrey

Worse adverse converse curse disburse disperse diverse hearse immerse intersperse inverse nurse purse rehearse reverse terse transverse traverse universe verse

W

Worst   burst cursed first nursed outburst thirst versed

Worth   birth dearth earth girth mirth

Would   brotherhood could fatherhood firewood good
Hollywood hood likelihood livelihood
misunderstood motherhood neighborhood
should sisterhood stood understood withstood
womanhood wood

Wound   (see **Sound**)

Woven   Beethoven cloven interwoven

Wow   allow avow bough bow brow chow cow disavow
endow frau how kowtow now ow plough plow
row slough somehow sow thou vow

Wrap   cap chap clap flap gap handicap lap map
mishap nap rap sap scrap slap snap strap tap
trap zap

Wrapper   capper clapper dapper flapper handicapper
rapper slapper snapper tapper whippersnapper
wiretapper yapper

Wrath   aftermath bath homeopath math path
psychopath sociopath

Wreck   check Czech deck fleck heck neck peck Quebec
speck trek

Wrecker   checker chequer decker double-decker
exchequer pecker woodpecker

Wrench   bench clench drench French monkey wrench
quench stench trench wench

Wrestle   nestle trestle vessel

W

Wretch   catch etch fetch kvetch retch sketch stretch wretch

Wring   (see **Sing**)

Wrinkle   crinkle periwinkle sprinkle tinkle twinkle

Wrist   (see **Mist**)

Write   appetite bite blight bright byte contrite copyright daylight delight despite dynamite excite Fahrenheit fight flight fright headlight height ignite invite kite knight light midnight might moonlight night outright parasite plight polite quite recite reunite right satellite sight site sleight slight spite starlight sunlight tight trite twilight unite white

Written   bitten Britain Briton kitten mitten smitten (see *in*)

Wrong   along belong bong ding-dong gong Hong Kong long Ping-Pong prong song strong throng

Wrote   afloat antidote bloat boat coat connote denote dote float footnote gloat goat misquote moat note oat overcoat promote quote remote riverboat rote smote throat tote underwrote vote

Wrought   (see **Thought**)

X

X-rated (see **Hated**)

X-ray array away bay betray bluejay bouquet bray clay day decay delay disarray dismay display eh? essay exposé fray gay gray hay hey holiday hooray José Kay lay matinee may moiré naysay negligée obey pay play portray protégé ray résumé ricochet risqué rosé say slay sleigh soufflé say stay stray sway they toupee way weigh

Xerox box chickenpox equinox fox mailbox orthodox ox paradox rocks socks stocks

Xylophone (see **Alone**)

Y

Yacht apricot blot Camelot clot cot cybot dot forget-me-not forgot fought gavotte got hot hot-shot jot knot lot not plot pot robot rot shot slingshot somewhat spot squat swat tot trot watt what

Yank bank blank clank crank dank drank flank frank hank outrank plank prank rank sank shrank spank stank tank thank

Yankee cranky hanky lanky

Yard avant-garde card chard discard disregard guard hard lard regard retard tarred

Yarn barn darn

Yawn Amazon Babylon begone bonbon Bonn brawn chiffon con Don dawn drawn fawn gone hexagon John lawn lexicon octagon on Oregon pawn pentagon silicon undergone upon withdrawn wanton

Year adhere appear atmosphere auctioneer beer bombardier career cashier cavalier chandelier cheer clear dear deer disappear ear engineer fear financier frontier gear hear hemisphere here insincere interfere jeer lavaliere leer mere mountaineer near overhear overseer peer persevere pioneer queer racketeer reappear rear revere seer severe shear sheer sincere smear sneer spear sphere stratosphere tear veneer volunteer

Yearn adjourn burn churn concern discern earn fern intern kern learn overturn return sojourn spurn stern taciturn turn urn

Yell bell belle Carmel carrousel cell clientele dell dwell excel farewell fell gel hell hotel infidel knell mademoiselle personnel sell shell smell spell tell well

Yellow bellow cello fellow hello mellow Othello

Yelp help kelp

Yes access address baroness bashfulness bitterness
bless caress chess cleverness cloudiness
compress confess craziness deadliness depress
digress distress dizziness dress duress
eagerness easiness eeriness emptiness excess
express finesse foolishness ghostliness guess
happiness haziness homelessness idleness
impress joyfulness joylessness laziness less
limitless Loch Ness lustfulness mess
nervousness obsess openness oppress
outrageousness penniless playfulness possess
press profess progress queasiness recess
regress repossess repress rockiness seediness
shallowness silkiness sleaziness sleepiness
sneakiness SOS spaciousness spitefulness
stress success suppress thoughtfulness
transgress uselessness viciousness willingness
wishfulness worldliness youthfulness

Yet alphabet bayonet bet brunette cabinet cadet
cigarette clarinet cornet corvette debt duet
epithet etiquette forget fret gazette get jet
Joliet Juliet let luncheonette marionette net
omelet pet quartet regret roulette set
silhouette Somerset sunset sweat threat Tibet
toilette upset vet 'vette violet wet

Yield battlefield Chesterfield field shield wield

Yodel modal nodal

Yoga Saratoga toga

Y

Yogurt (see **Shirt**)

Yoke (see **Joke**)

Yonder condor conned 'er fonder launder ponder squander wander

You adieu anew avenue barbecue bayou chew choo-choo cue curfew debut dew due ensue ewe few guru honeydew hue I.O.U. imbue ingénue interview Jew knew lieu new Nehru overdue pee-ewe pew preview pursue renew residue revenue review spew subdue sue undue view yew (see *do*)

Young among clung dung flung high-strung hung lung rung slung sprung strung stung sung swung tongue unstrung unsung wrung

Your (see **Door**)

Your allure armature assure brochure caricature cocksure cure demure endure ensure expenditure immature impure insecure insure liqueur literature lure manicure manure mature miniature obscure overture pedicure premature pure reassure secure signature sure tablature temperature

Yourself elf herself himself itself myself self shelf

Youth booth couth Duluth sleuth tooth truth uncouth

Yum album aquarium auditorium become bum burdensome Christendom come cranium

crematorium crumb curriculum drum dump
emporium fee-fi-fo-fum glum gum gymnasium
hum kettledrum kingdom martyrdom
maximum meddlesome medium millennium
minimum mum museum numb opium
overcome pendulum petroleum platinum plum
premium quarrelsome radium random rum
sanitarium scum slum some strum succumb
sum swum tedium thumb Tom Thumb
Tweedledum uranium worrisome yum

Yuppie guppy puppy

Z

Zany brainy grainy rainy

Zap cap chap clap flap gap handicap lap map
mishap nap rap sap scrap slap snap strap tap
trap wrap

Zeal (see **Wheel**)

Zealous jealous sell us tell us (see *us*)

Zebra duh Ophra (see *raw*)

Zen amen citizen den fen hen hydrogen Ken oxygen
pen regimen specimen ten then yen

Zinc blink brink chink clink drink fink ink kink link
mink pink rink shrink sink slink stink think wink

Zip battleship chip clip dip drip equip flip grip gyp
hip lip nip quip rip scrip ship slip snip strip tip
trip whip

Z

Zit befit bit fit 'git grit kit knit hit it lit mitt nit-wit pit
quit sit twit unfit ultimate wit zit

Zodiac (see **Track**)

Zone alone atone backbone baritone blown bone
chaperone clone condone cone cornerstone
cyclone Dictaphone flown full-blown full-grown
gramophone grindstone groan grown
headstone known loan lone microphone
milestone moan monotone mown overgrown
overthrown own phone postpone prone
saxophone sewn shown stone telephone
thrown tone trombone unknown xylophone
zone

Zoo accrue ado bamboo blew blue boo boohoo brew
caribou cashew clue construe coo coup crew
cuckoo do drew flew flue glue gnu goo grew
Hindu hitherto hullabaloo igloo impromptu
into issue Kalamazoo kangaroo kazoo kickapoo
misconstrue moo outdo overdo overthrew
peekaboo Peru poo rendezvous screw shampoo
shoe shoo shrew Sioux slew slue stew taboo
tattoo threw through tissue to too true two
undo voodoo wahoo well-to-do who withdrew
woo yahoo zoo Zulu (see *you*)

Zoom bloom boom broom cloakroom doom entomb
flume gloom groom room tomb whom womb

Z